I0701641

Presents

Black Love

Adult Coloring Book

This Book Belongs To:

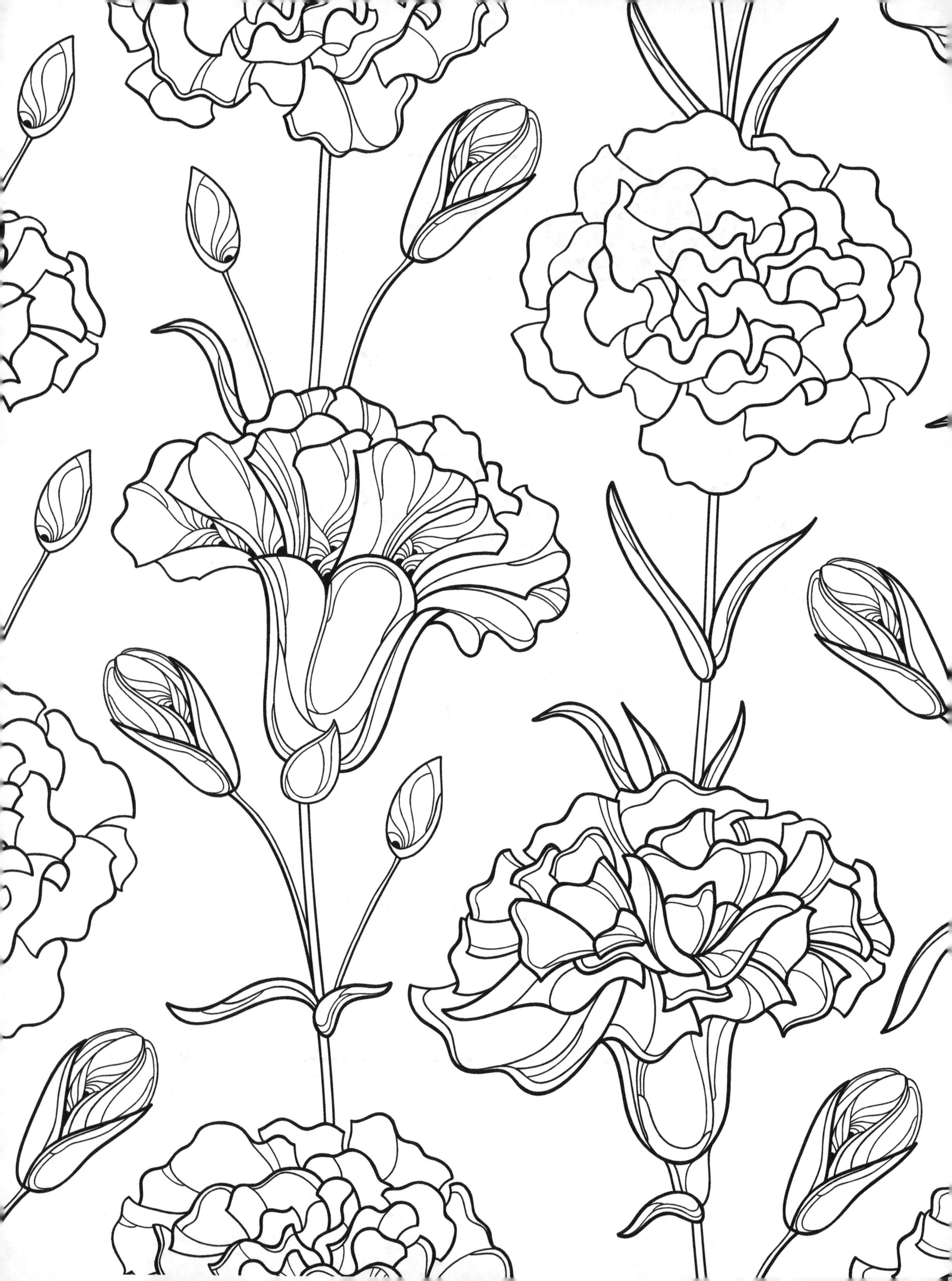

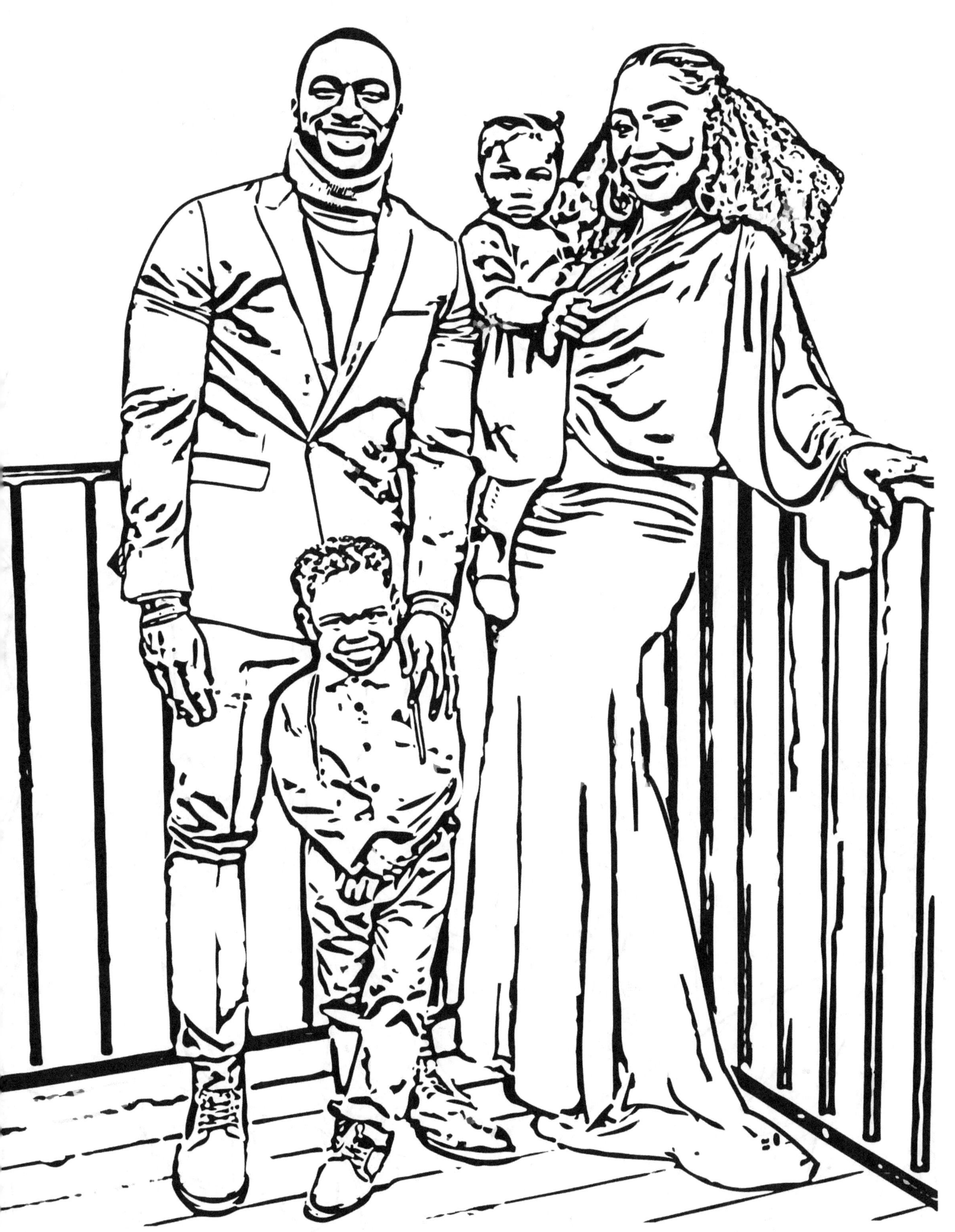

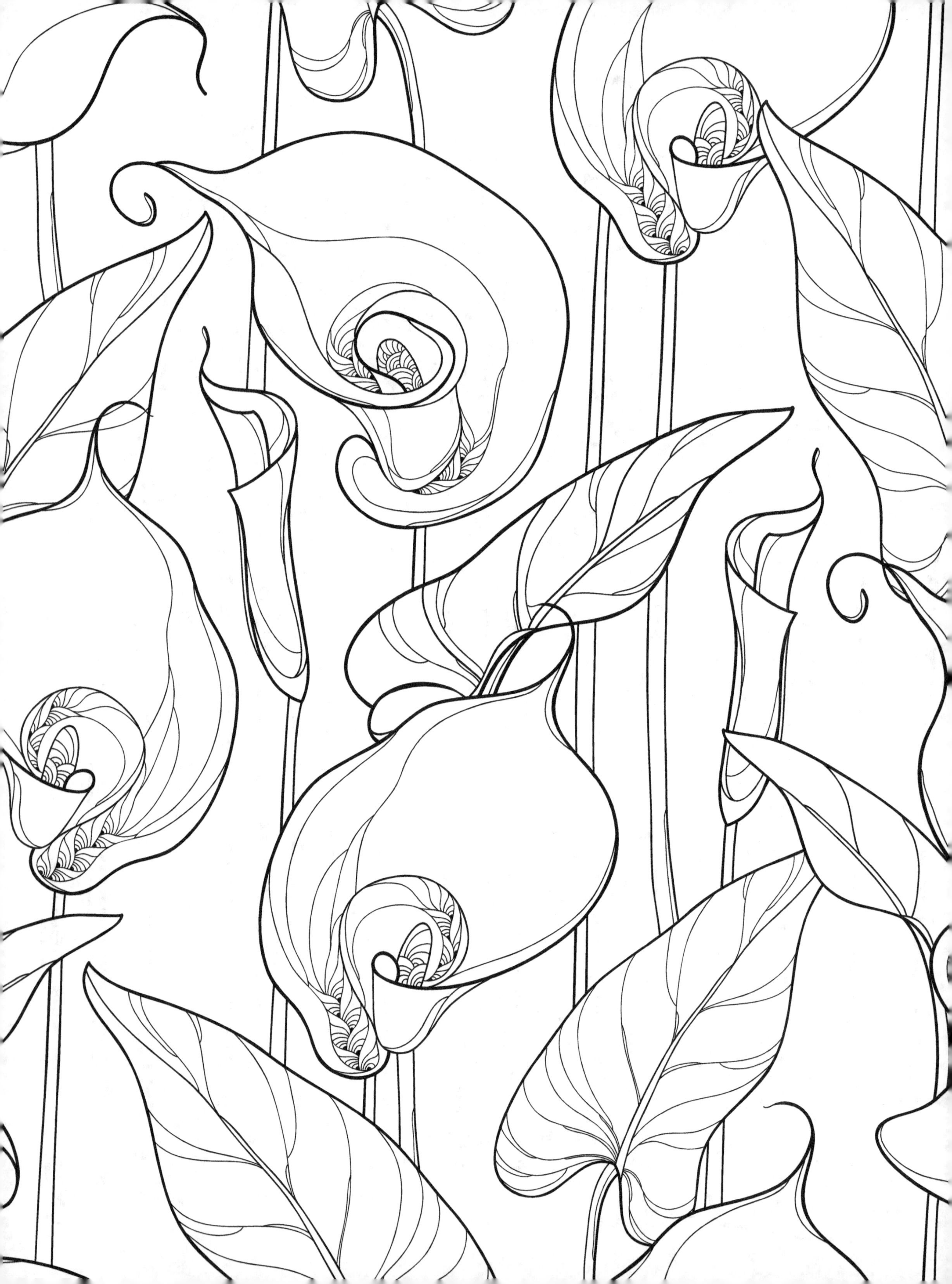

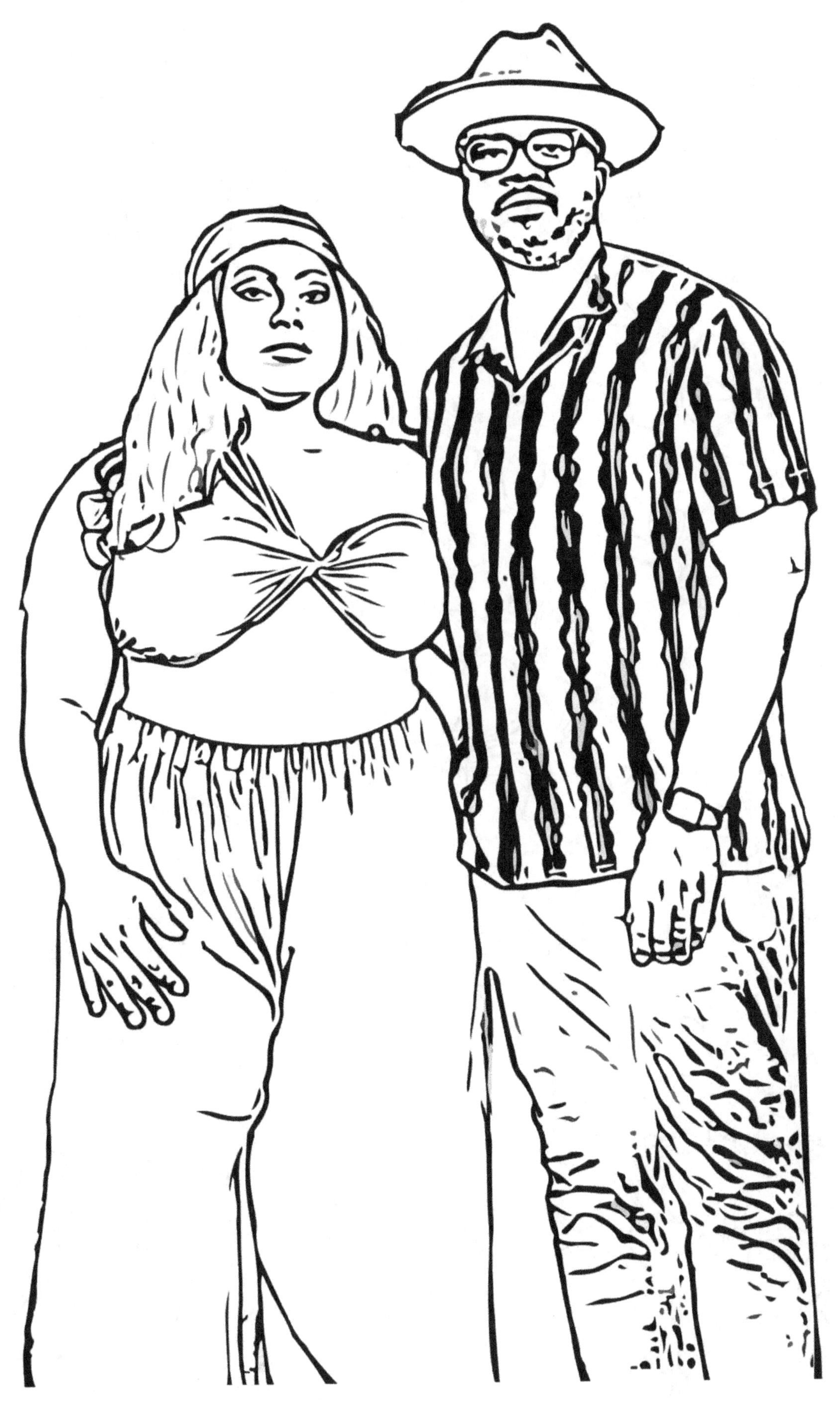

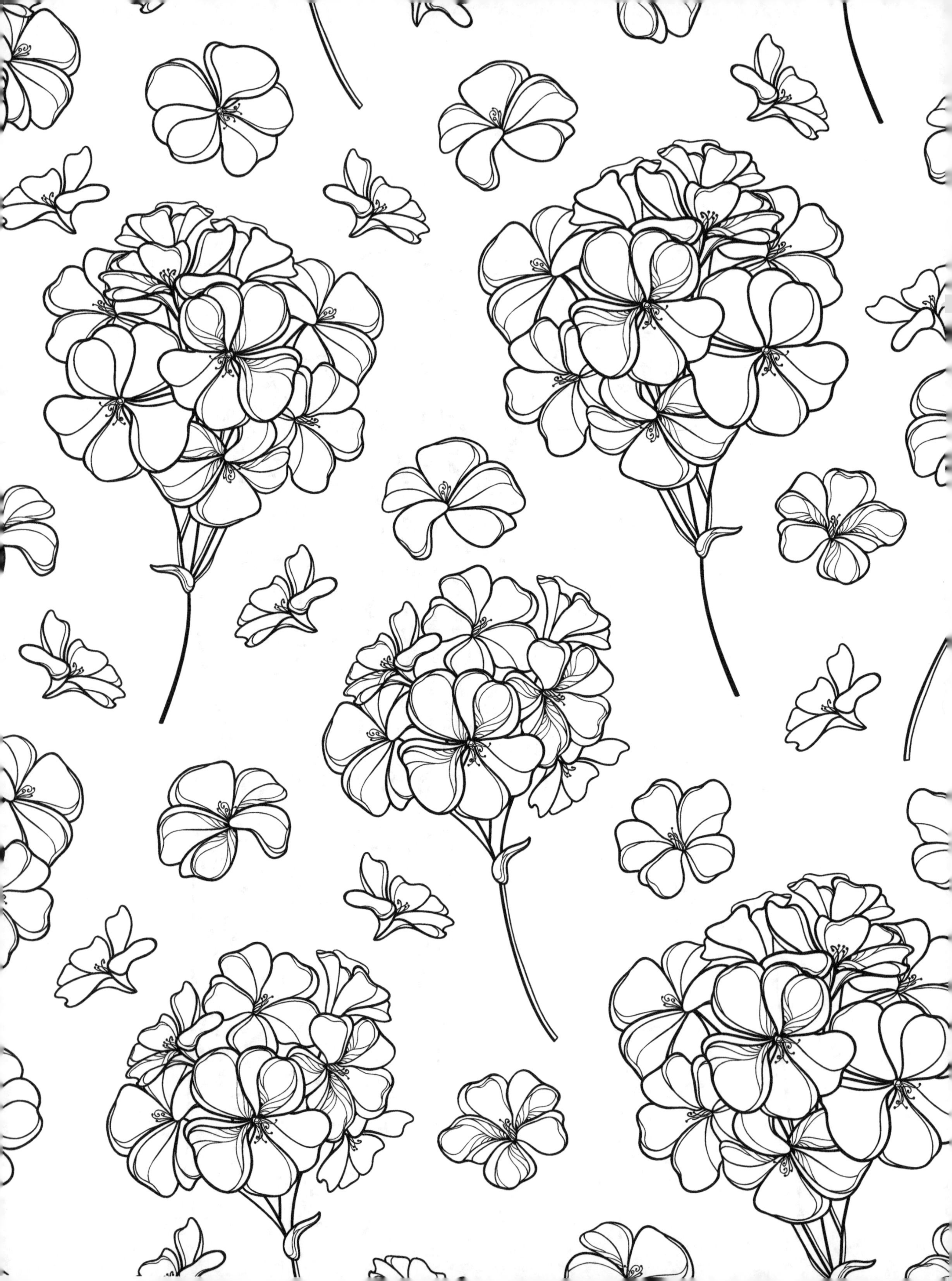

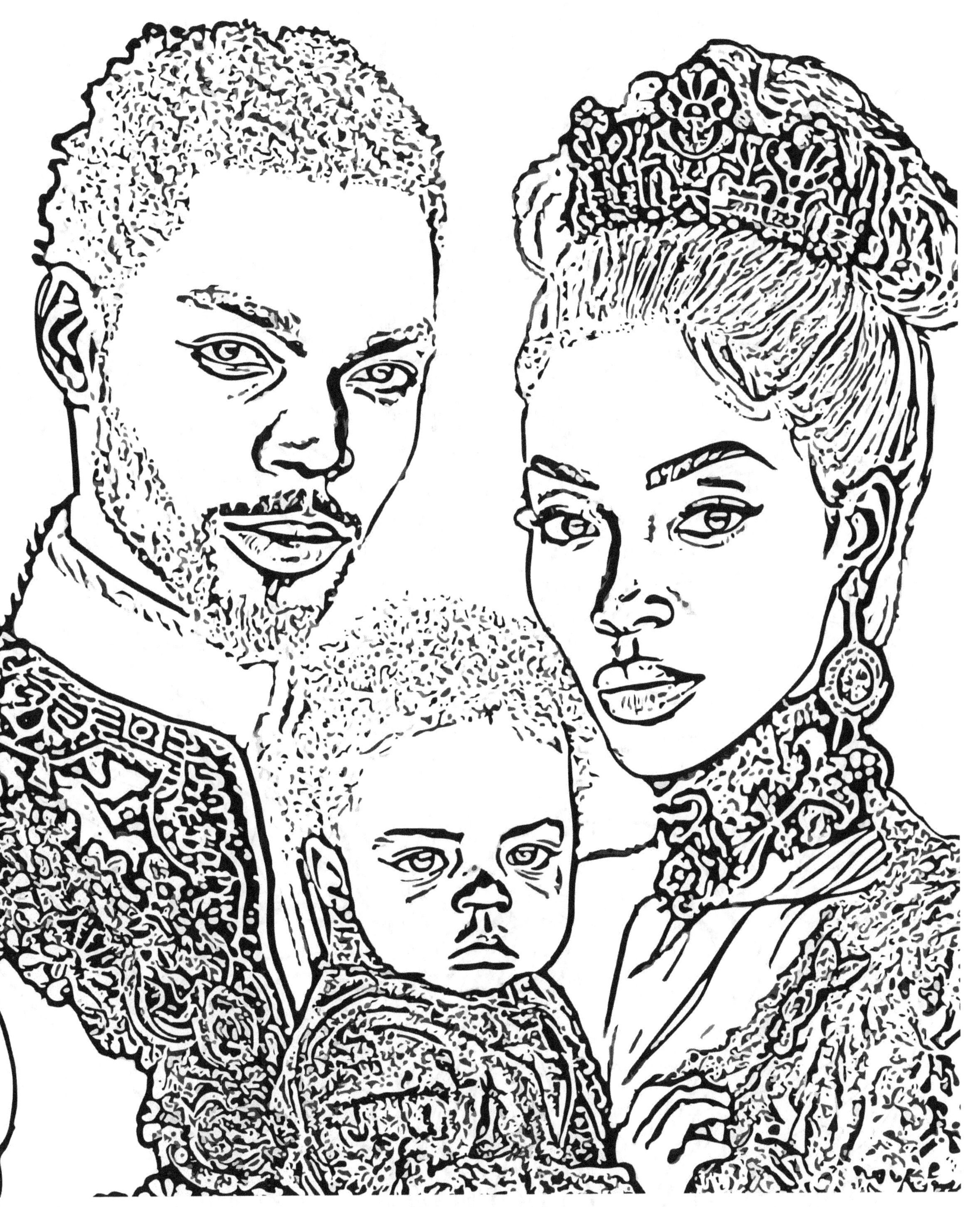

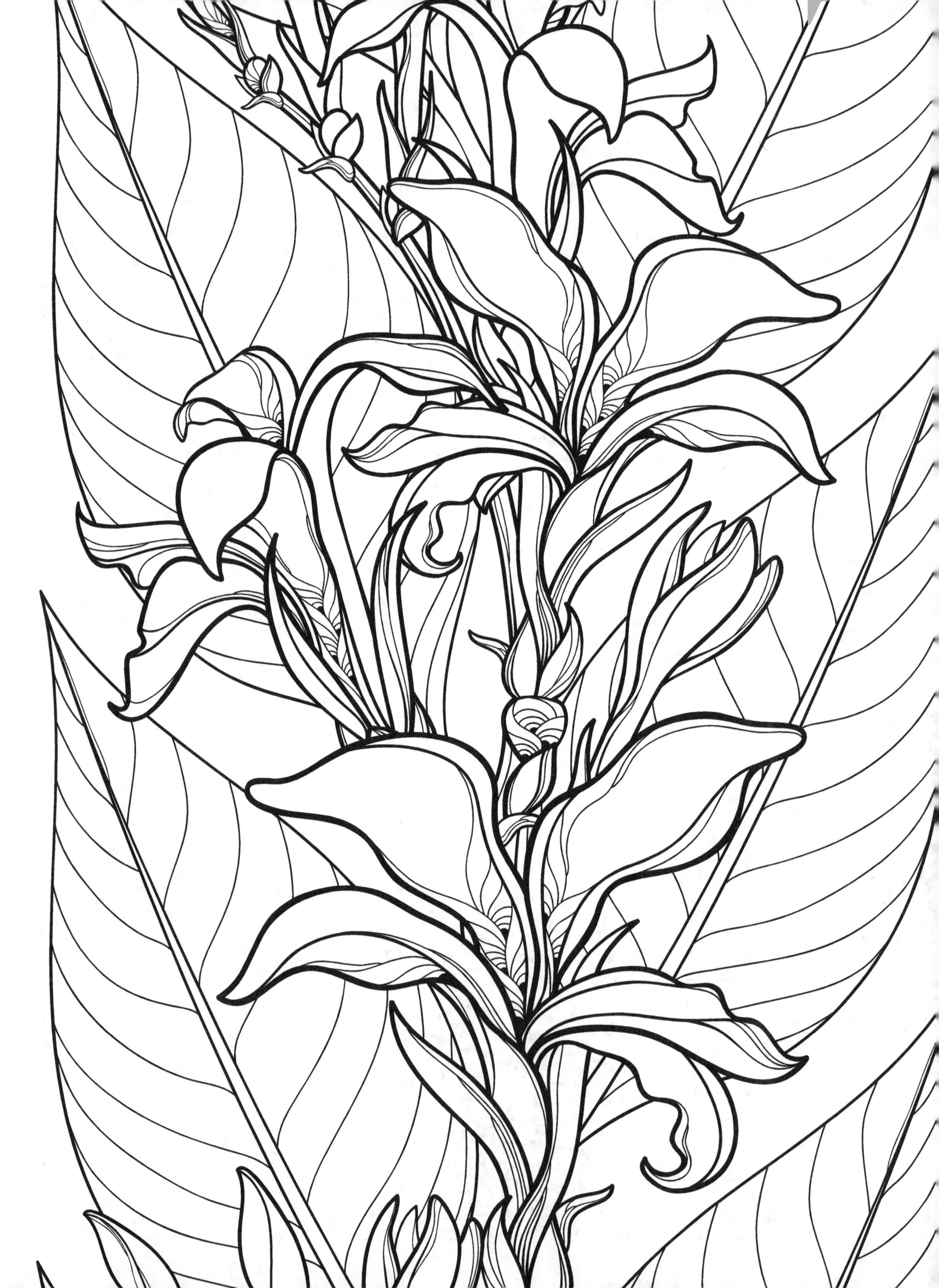

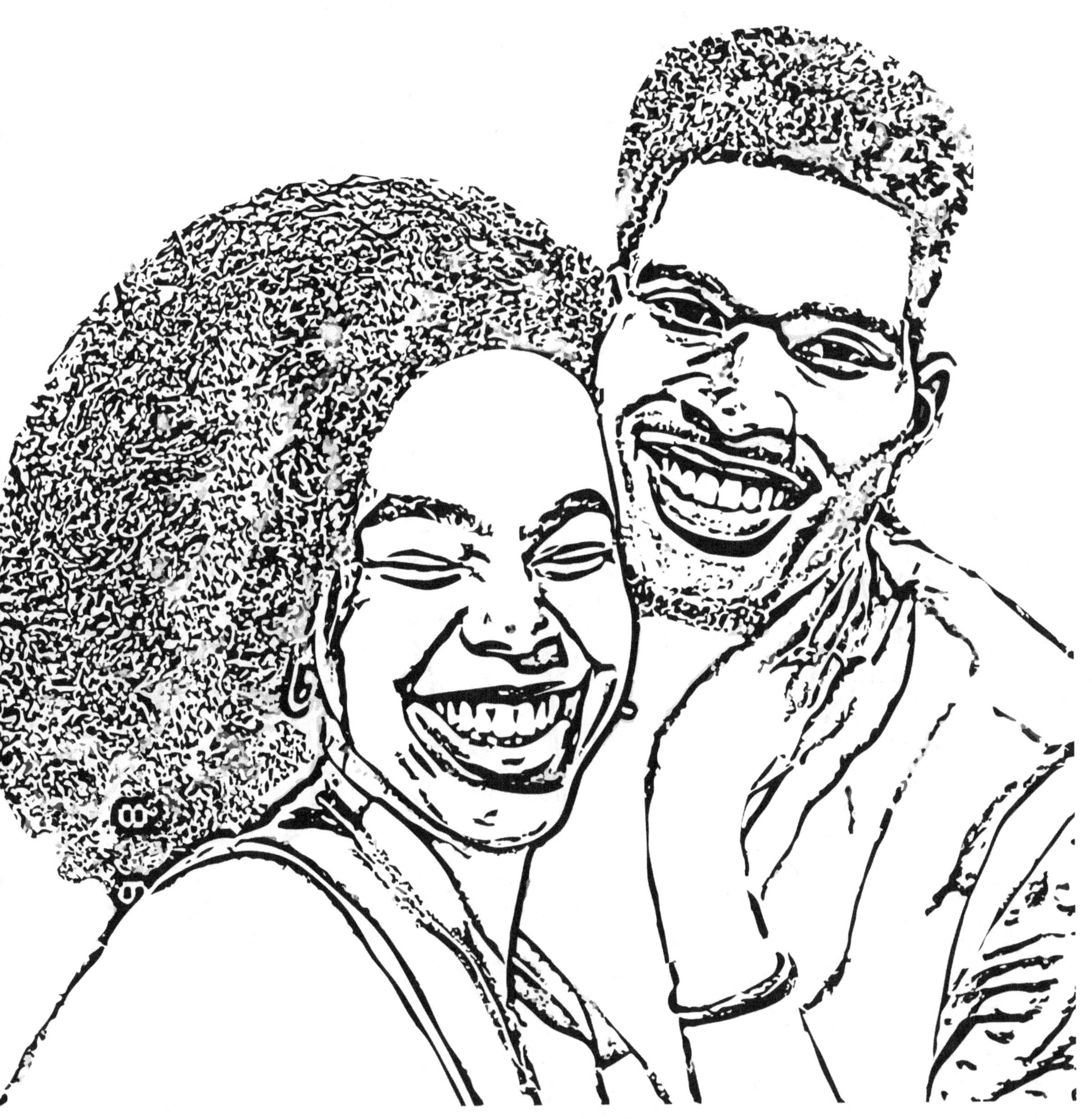

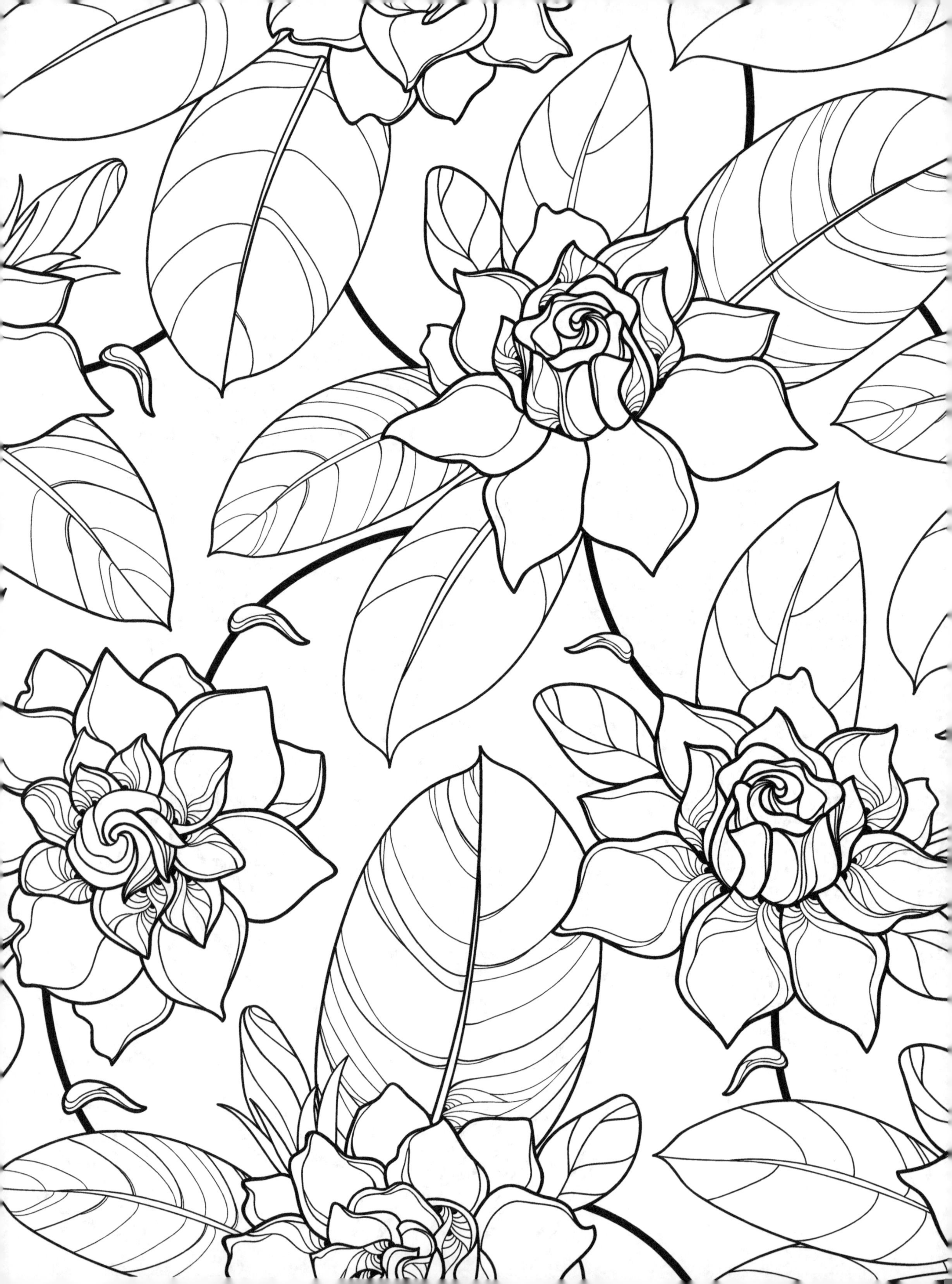

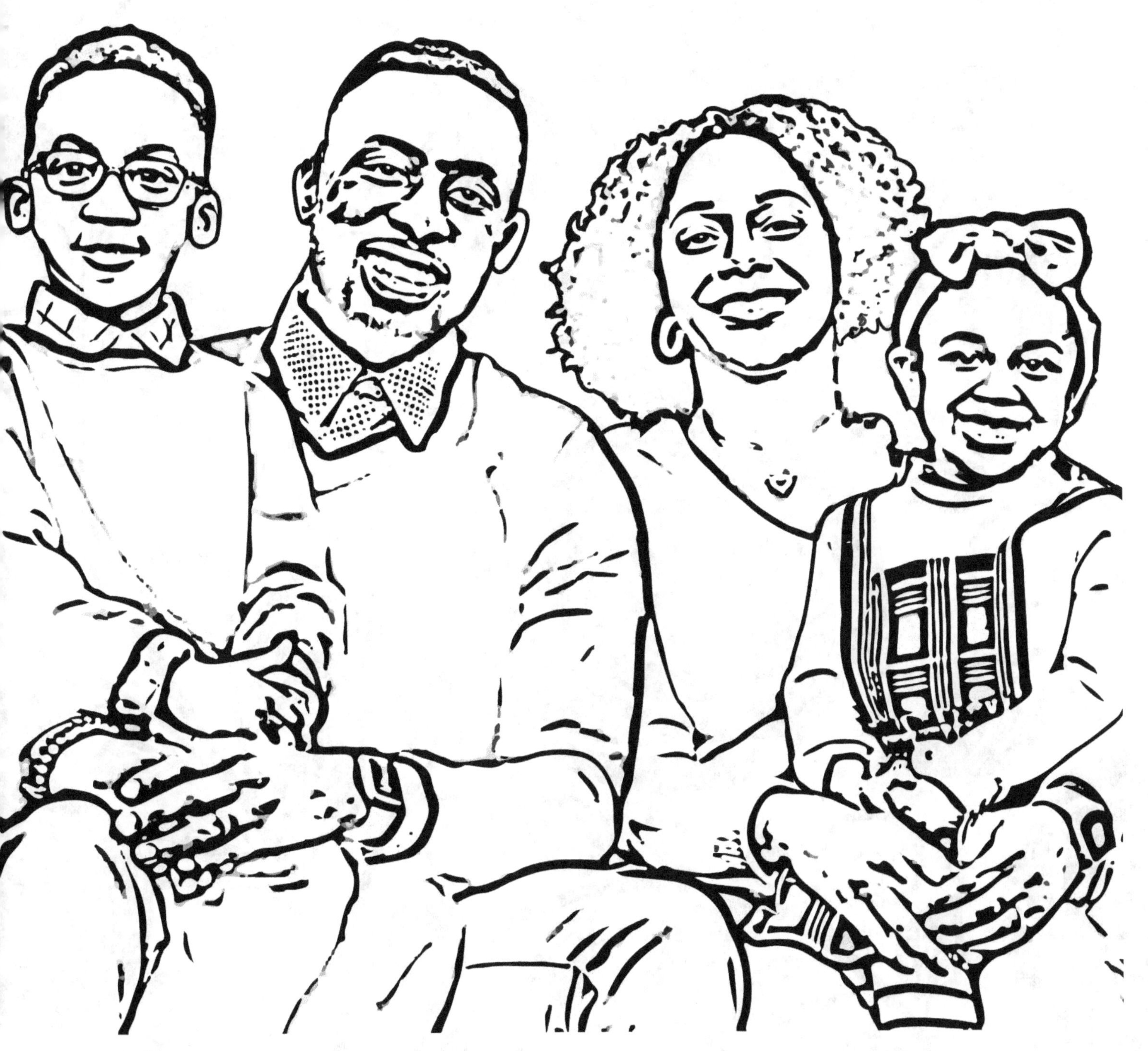

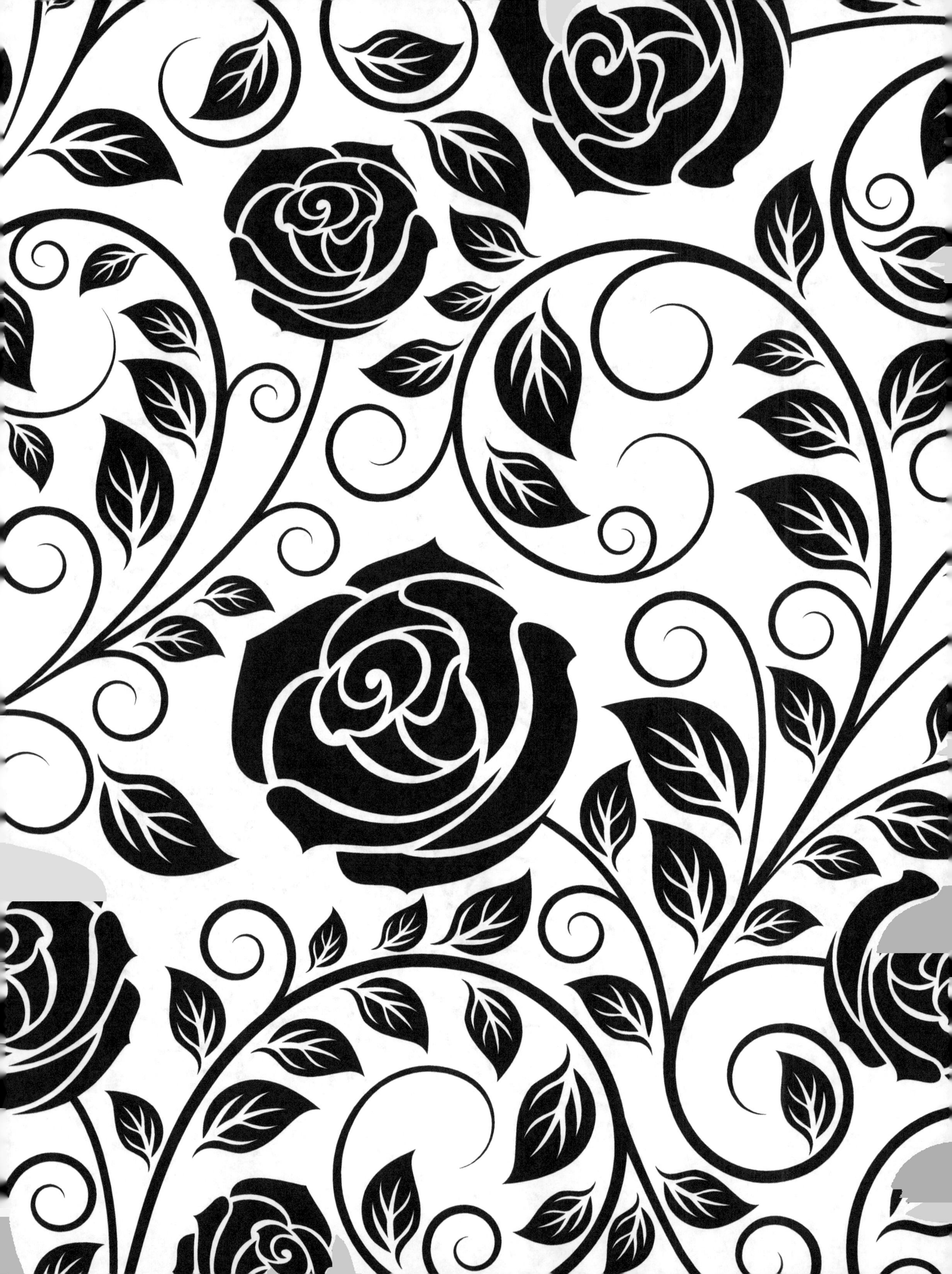

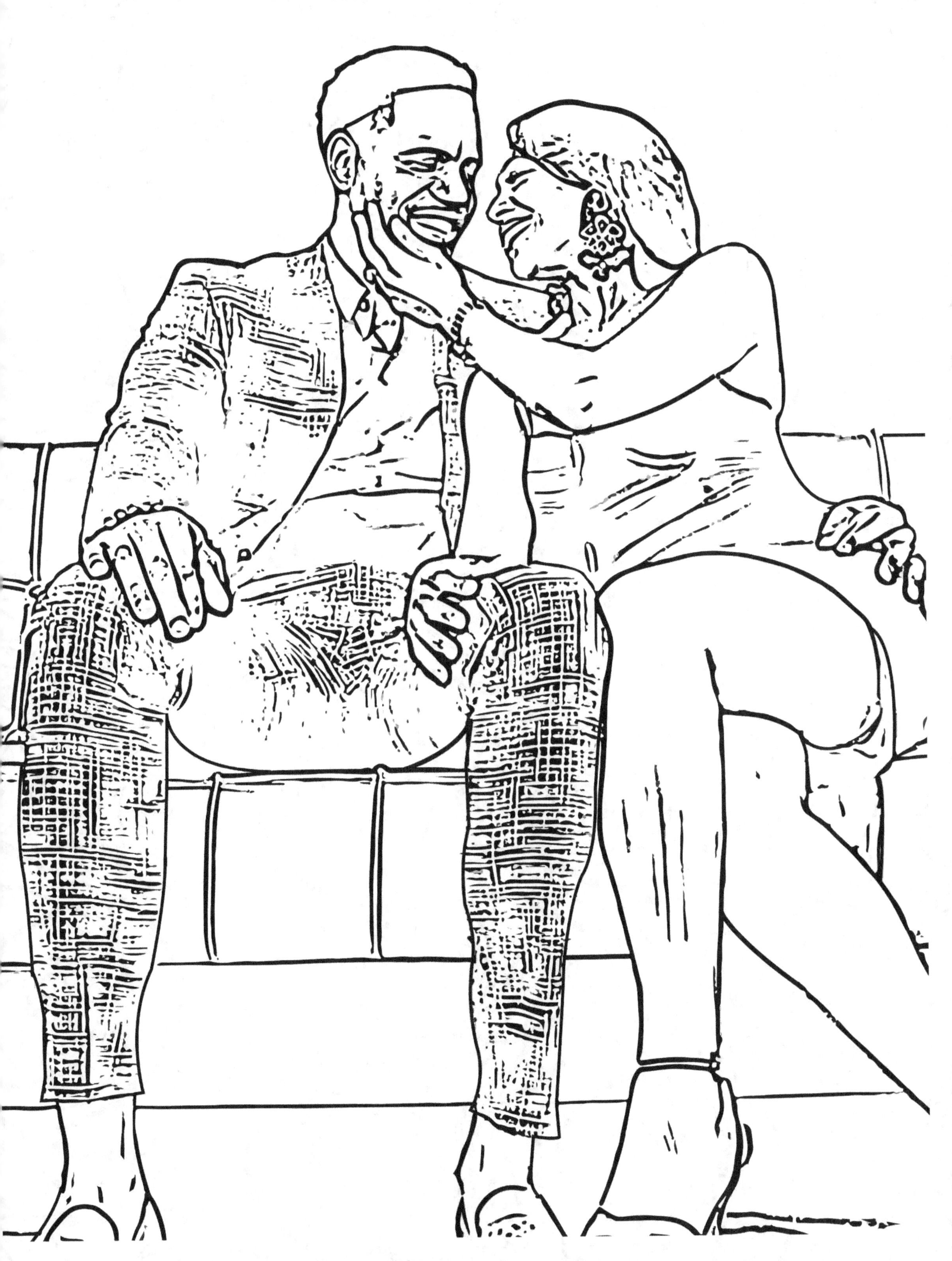

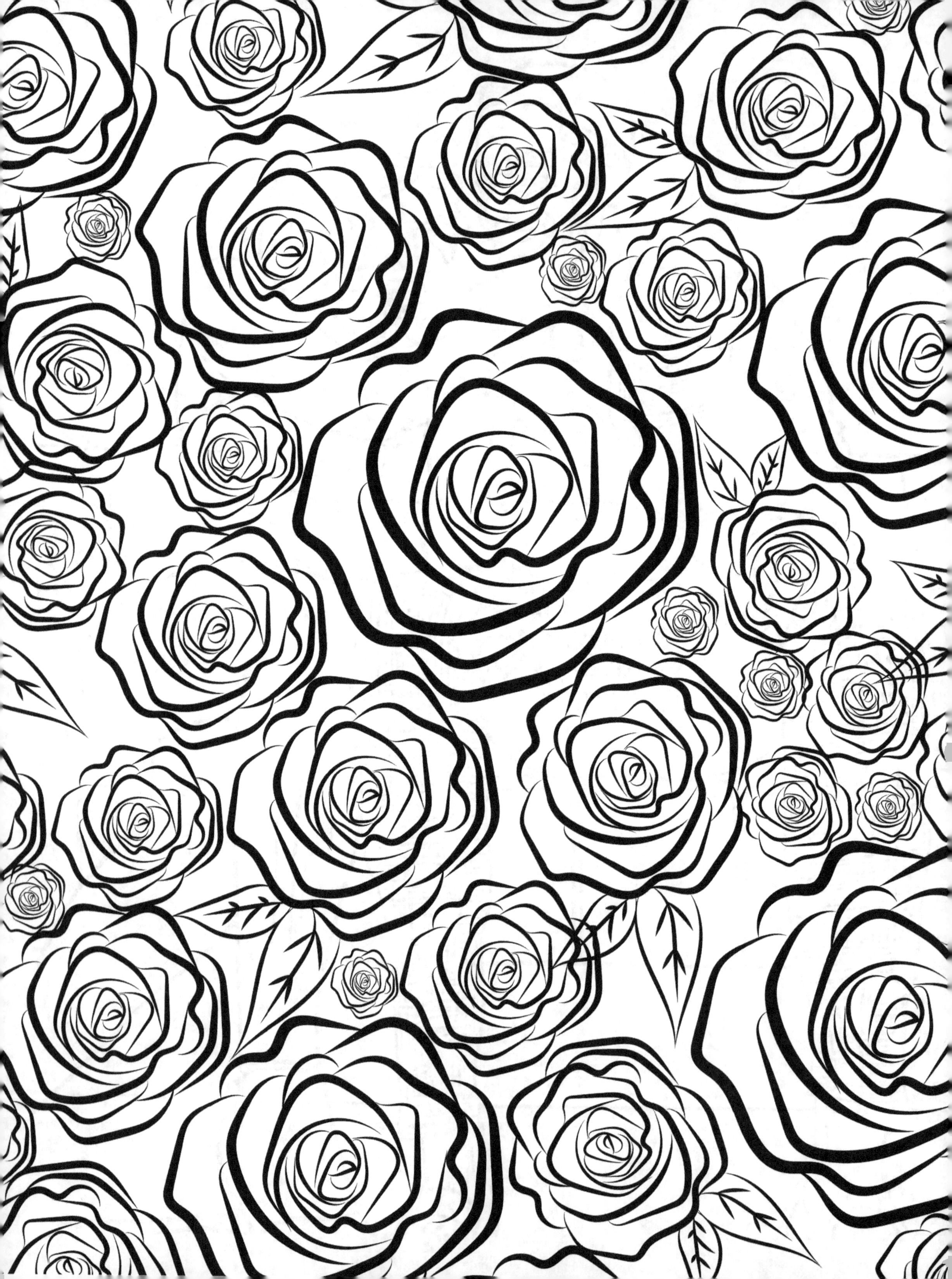

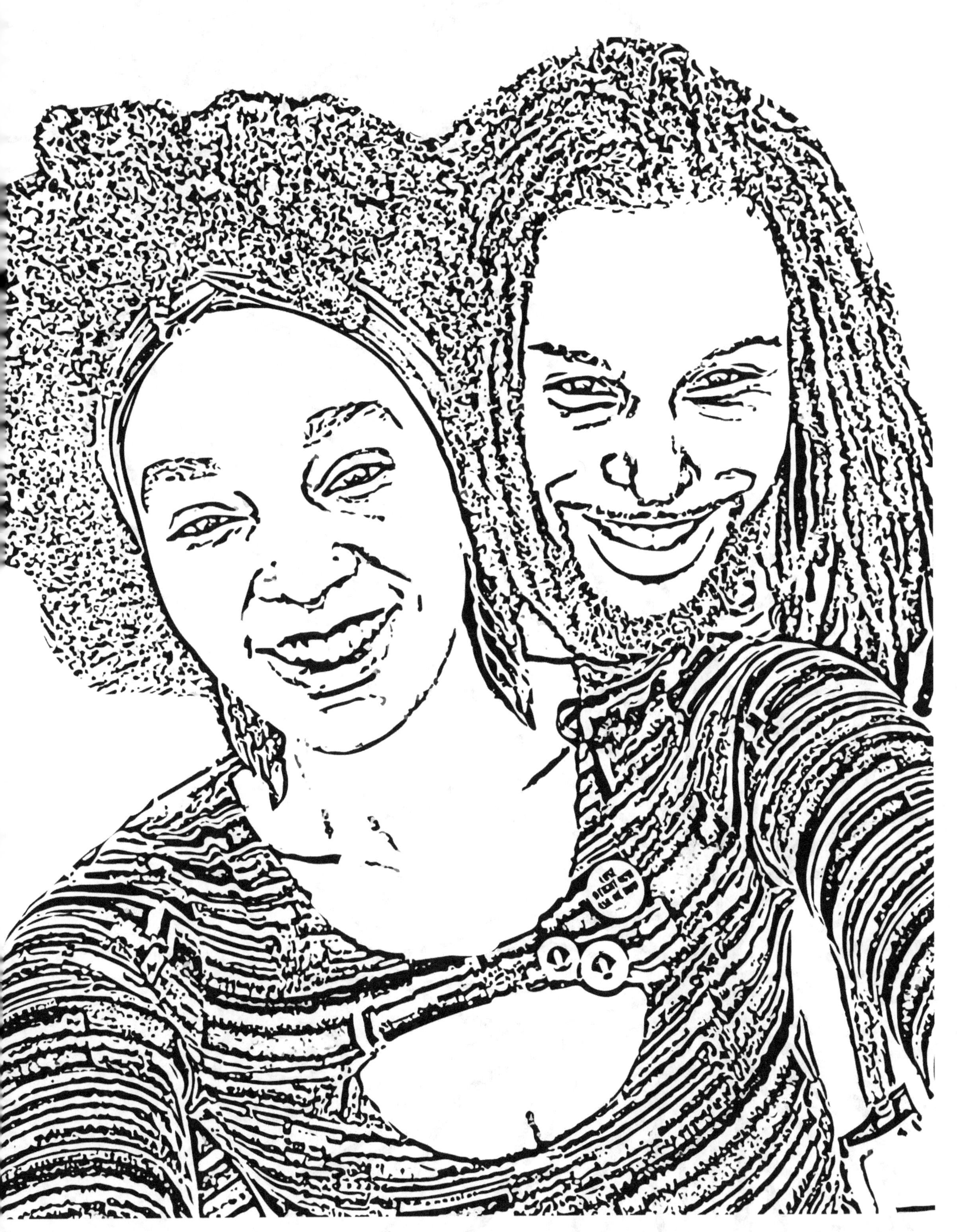

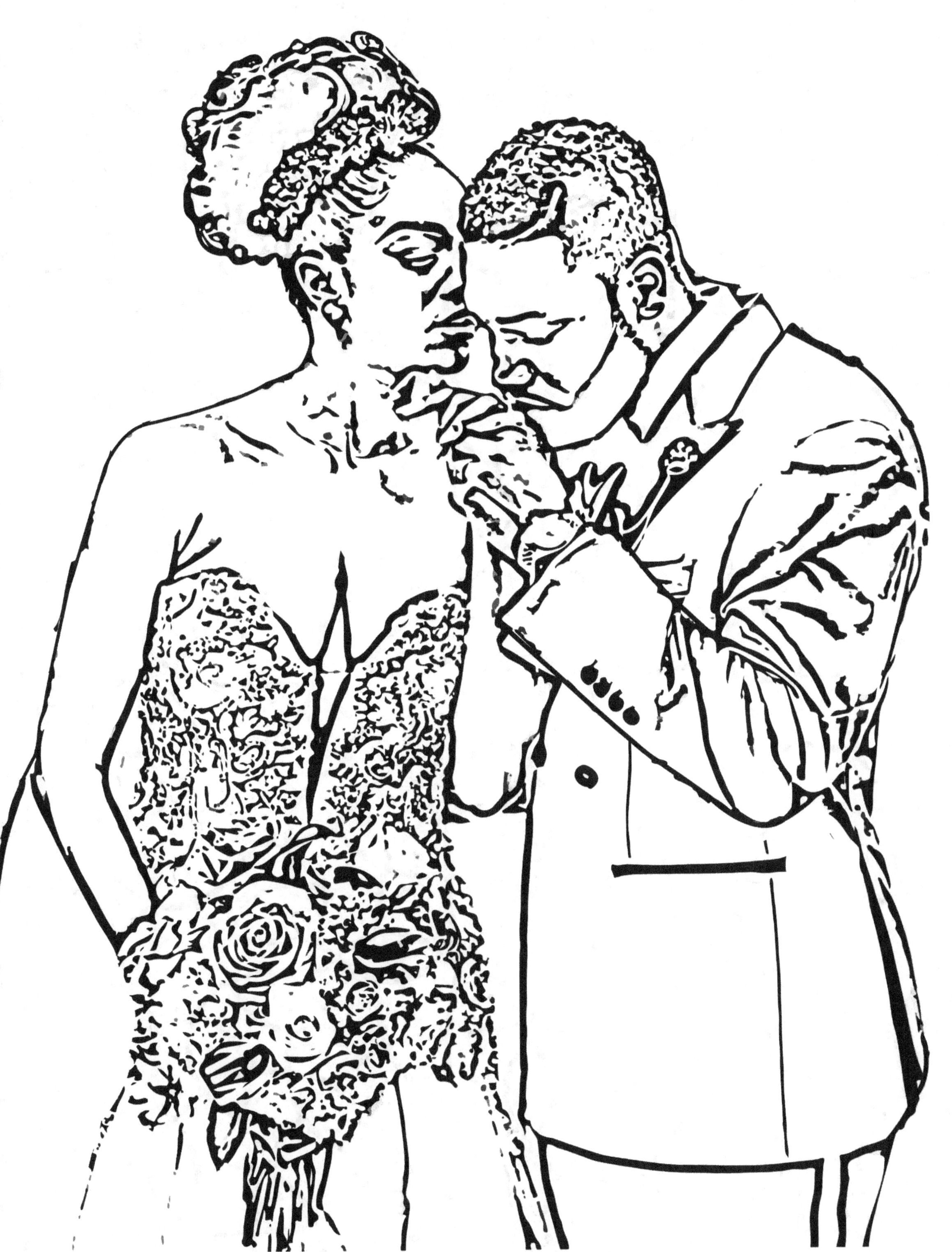

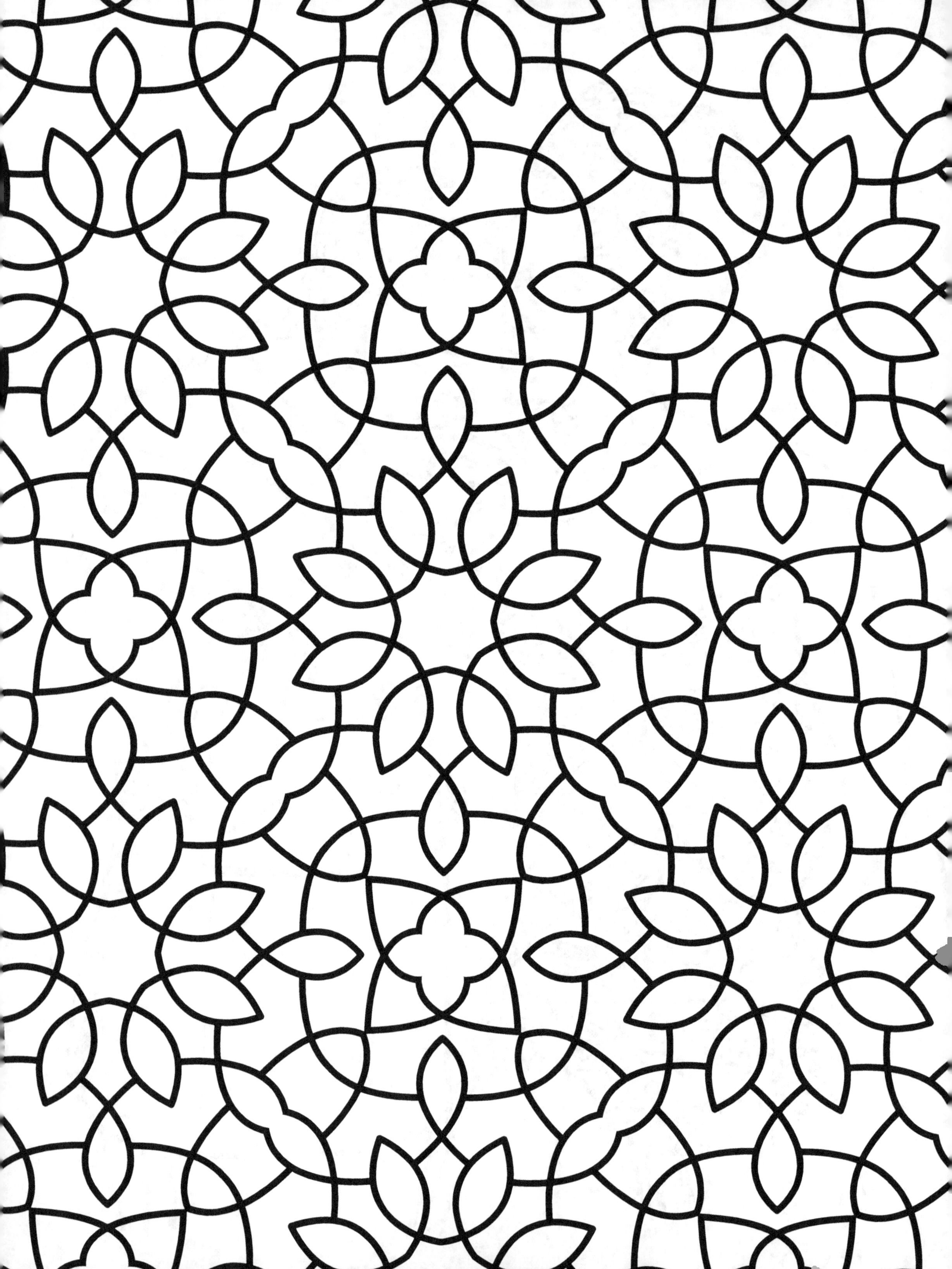

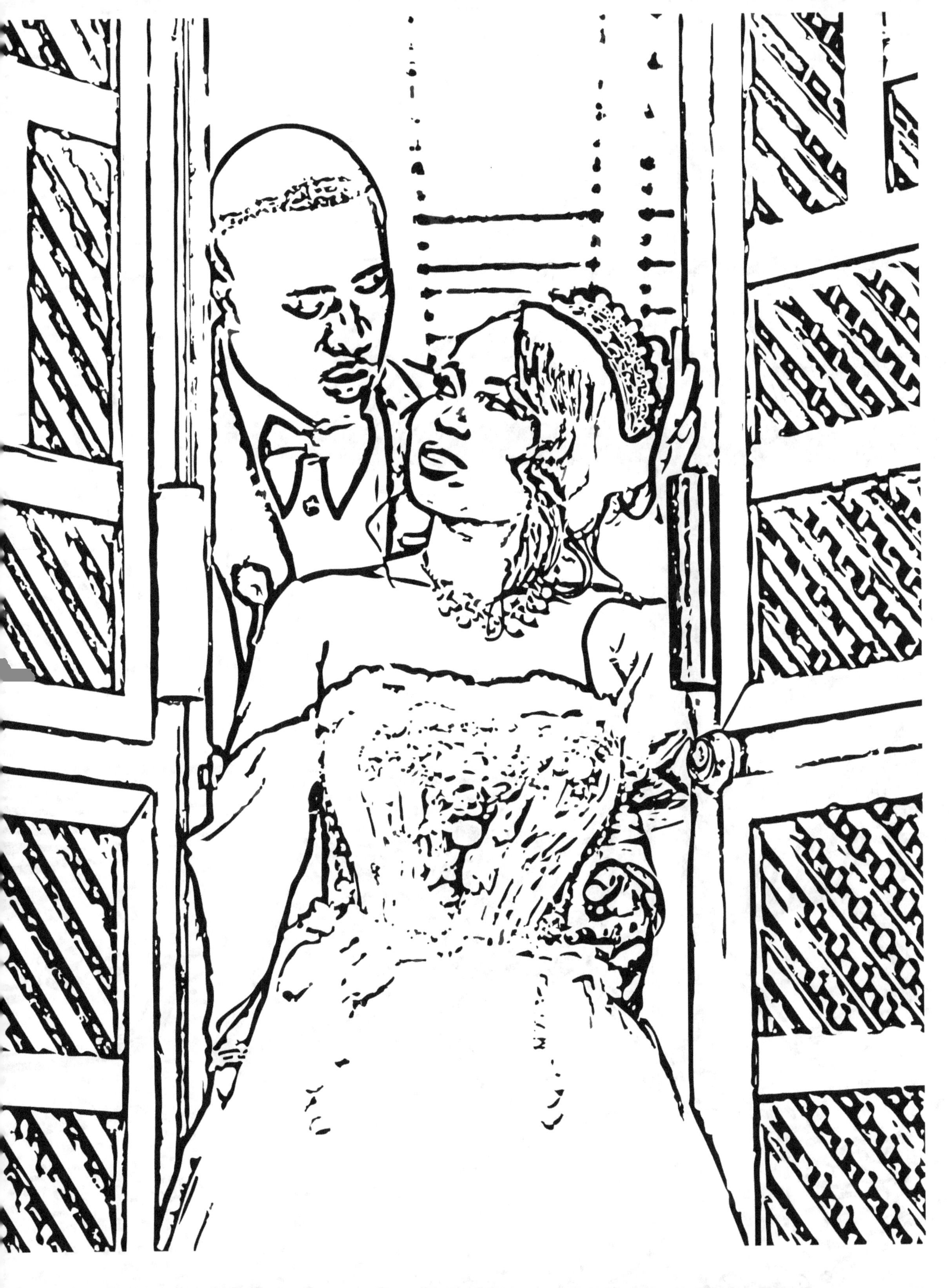

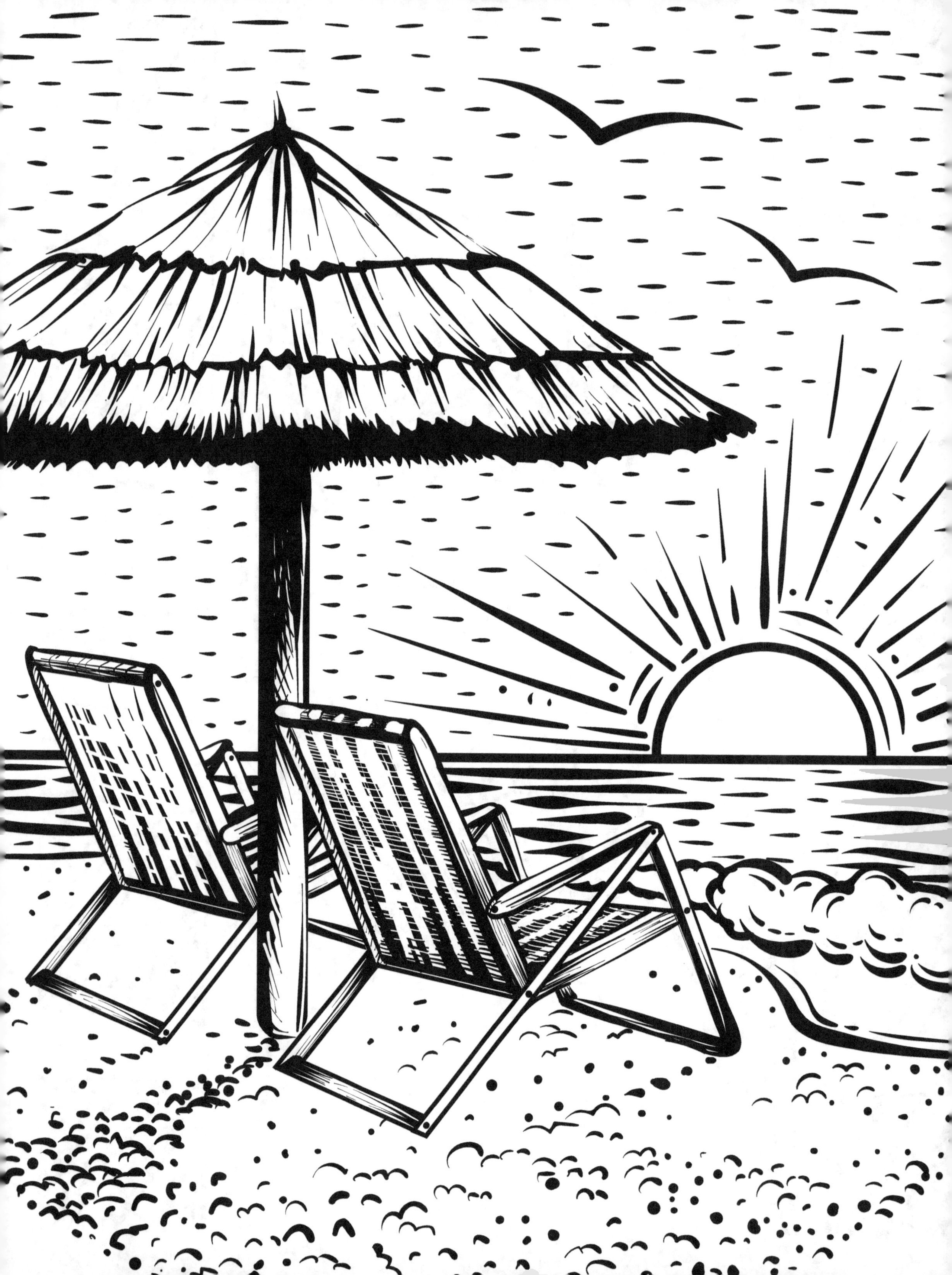

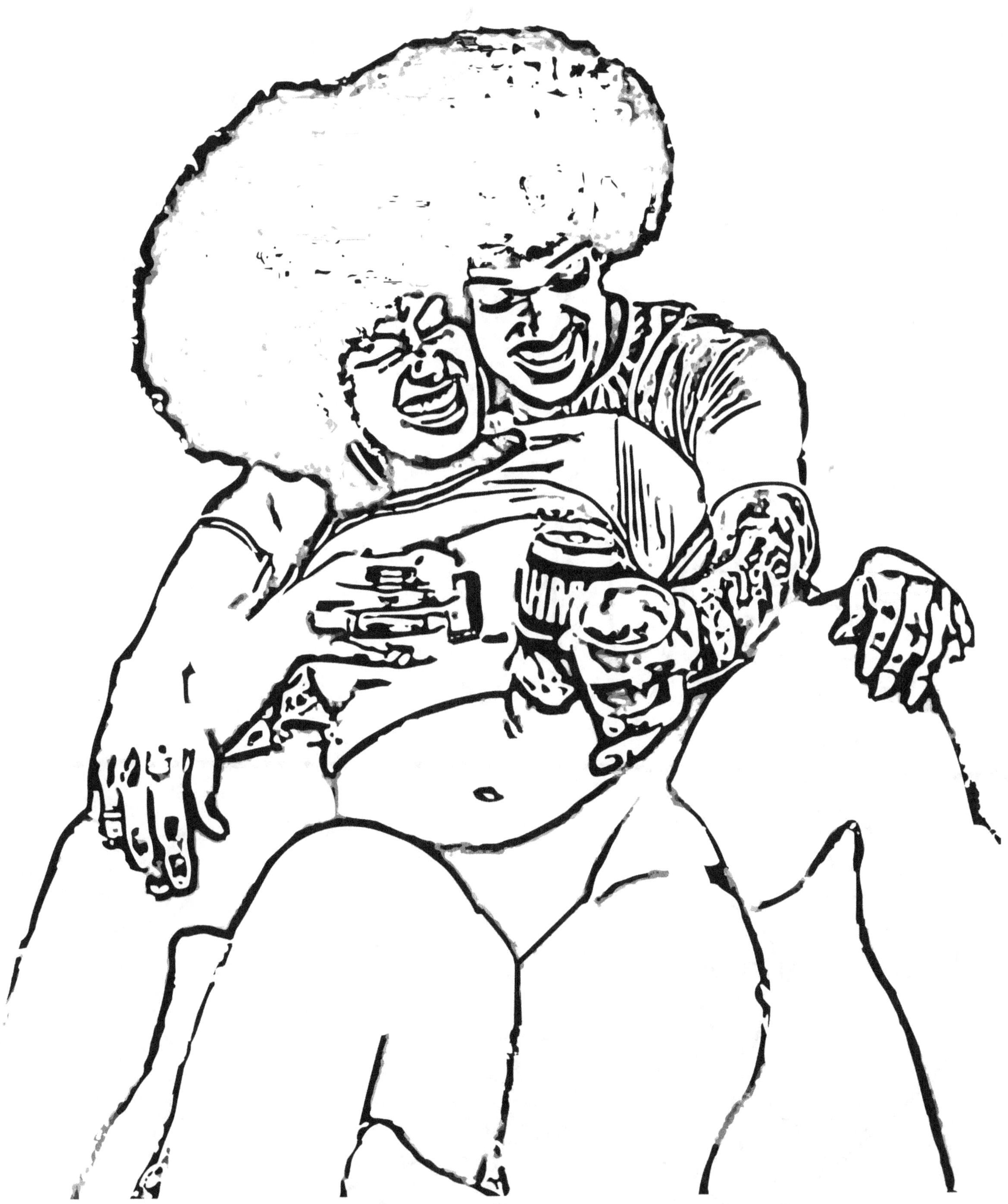

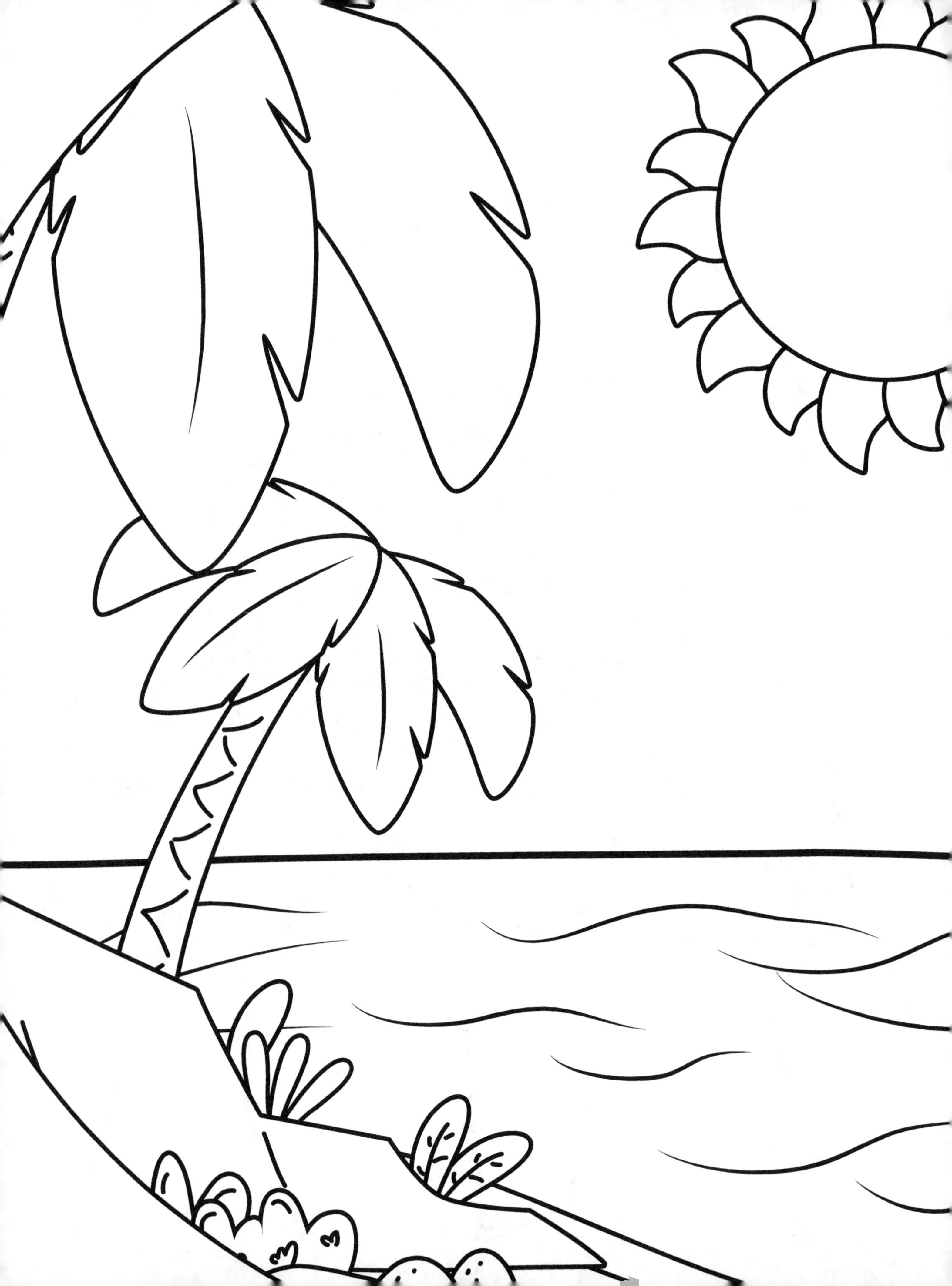

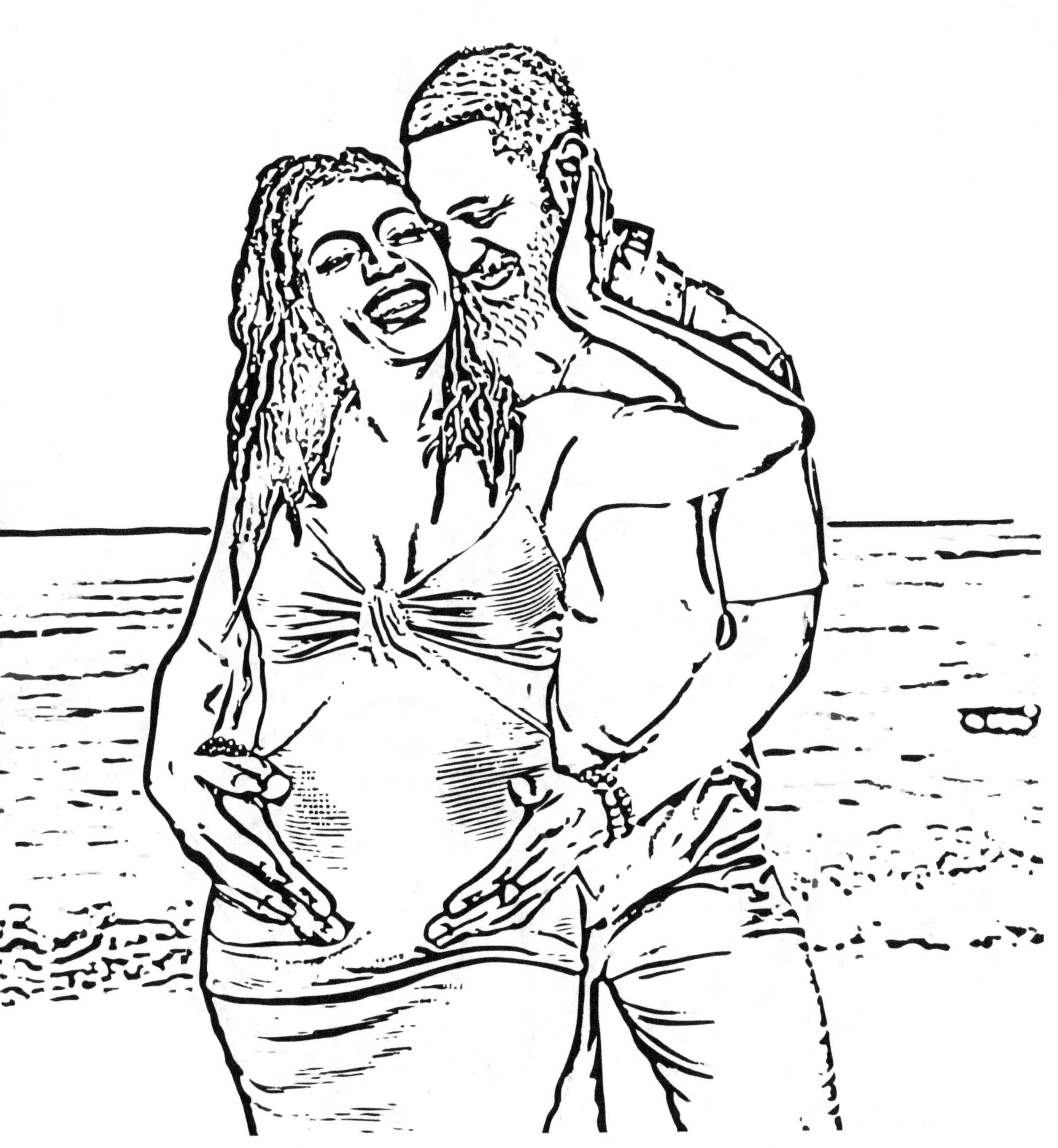

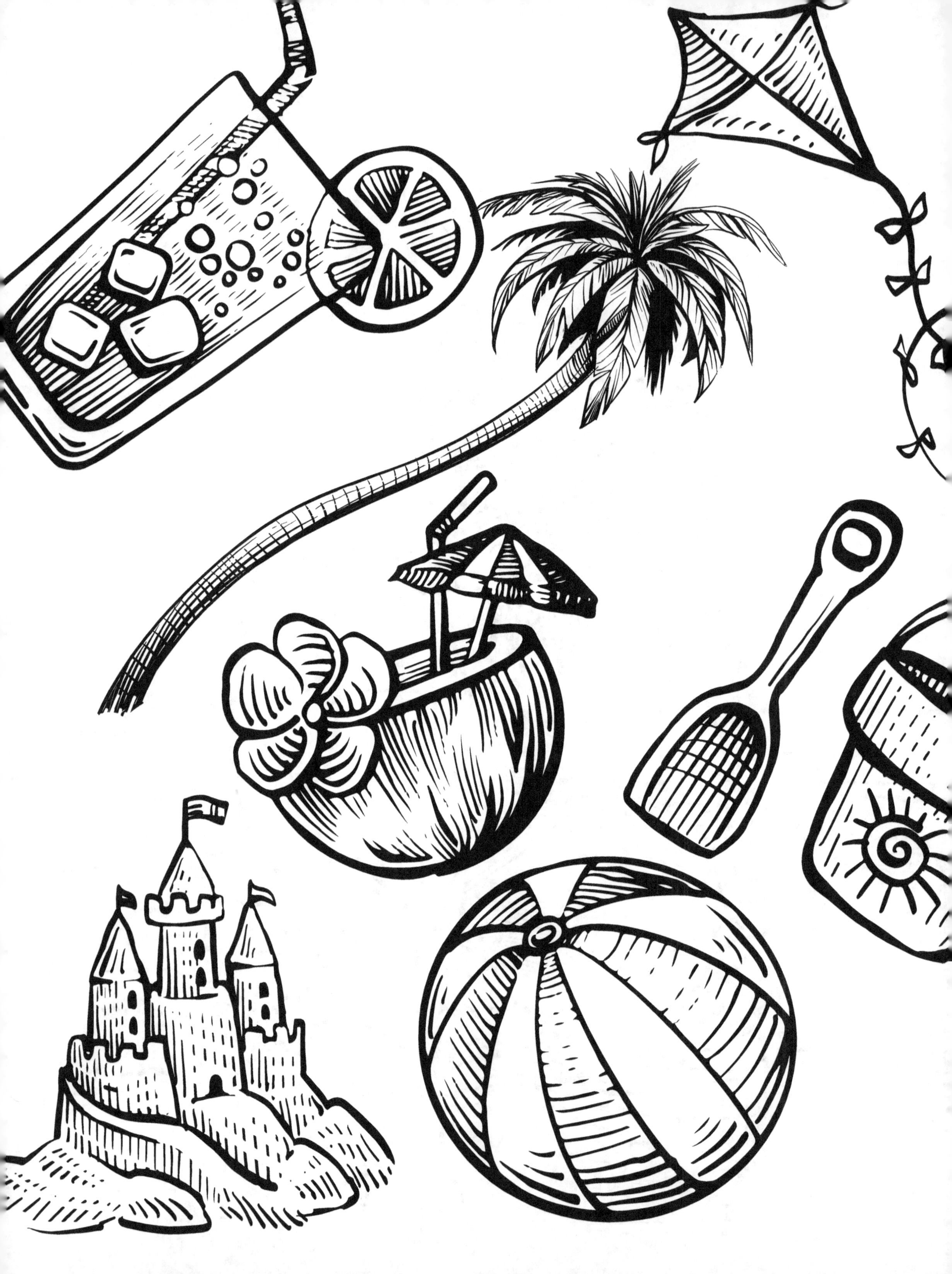

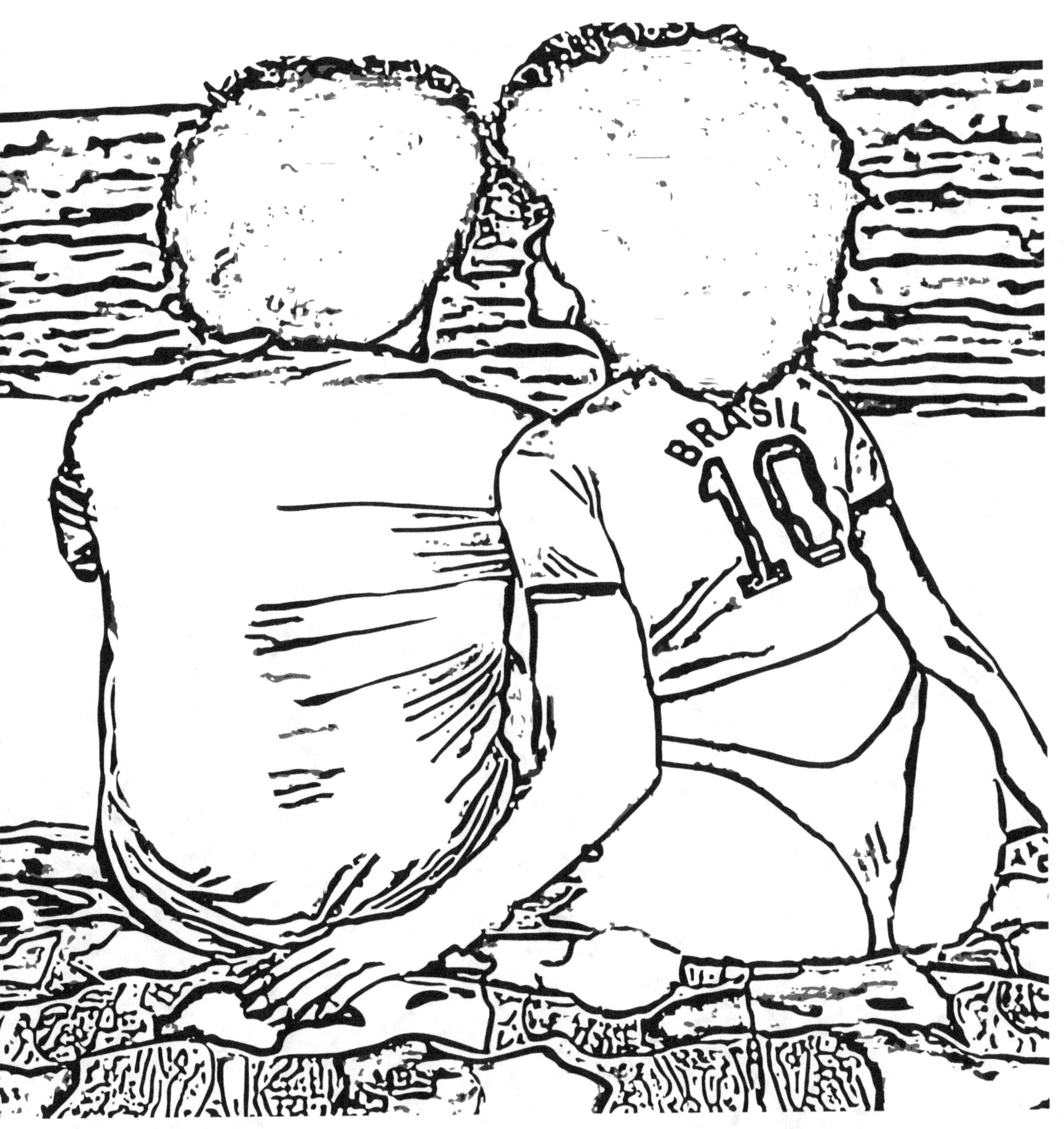
BRASIL
10

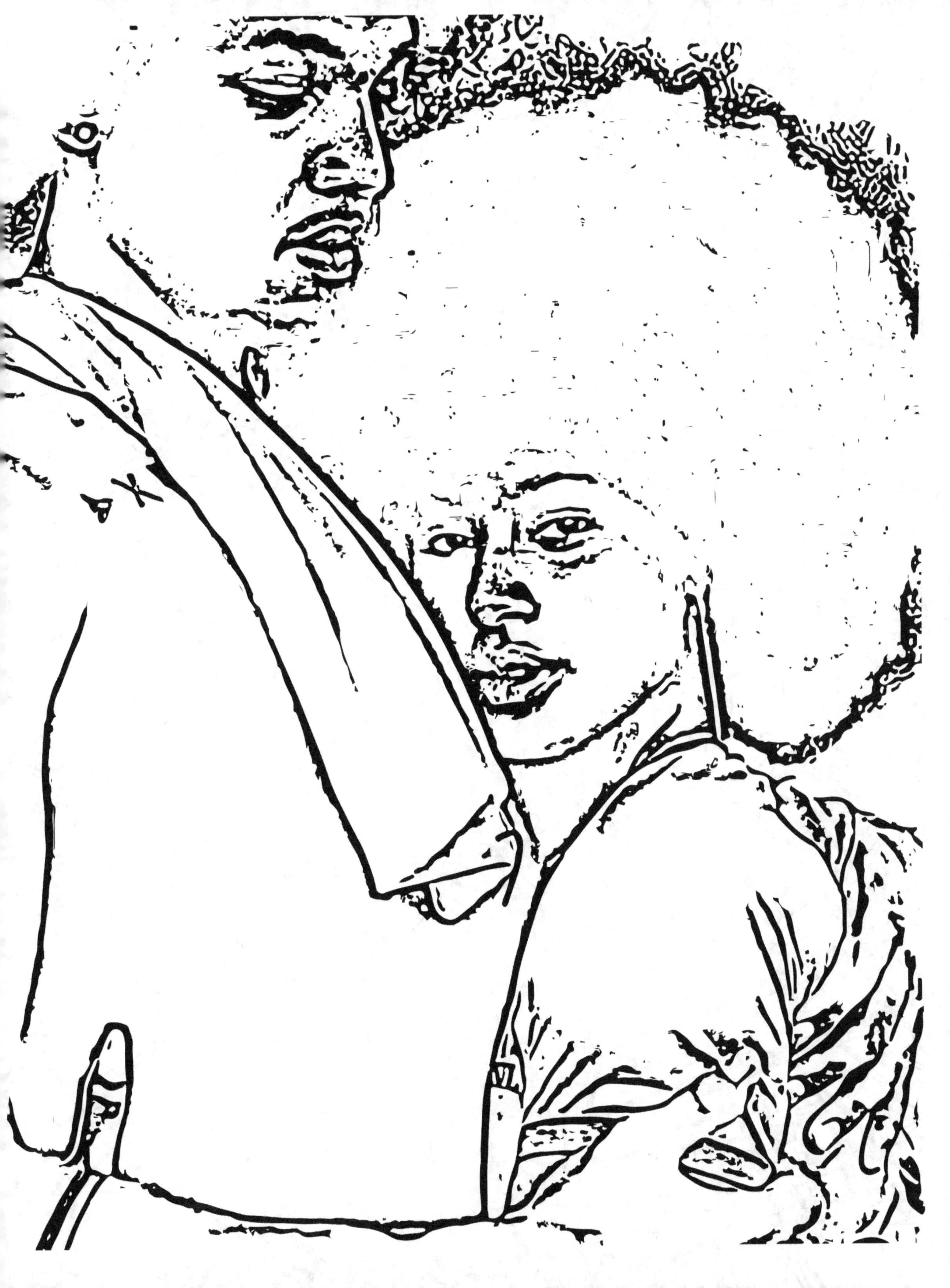

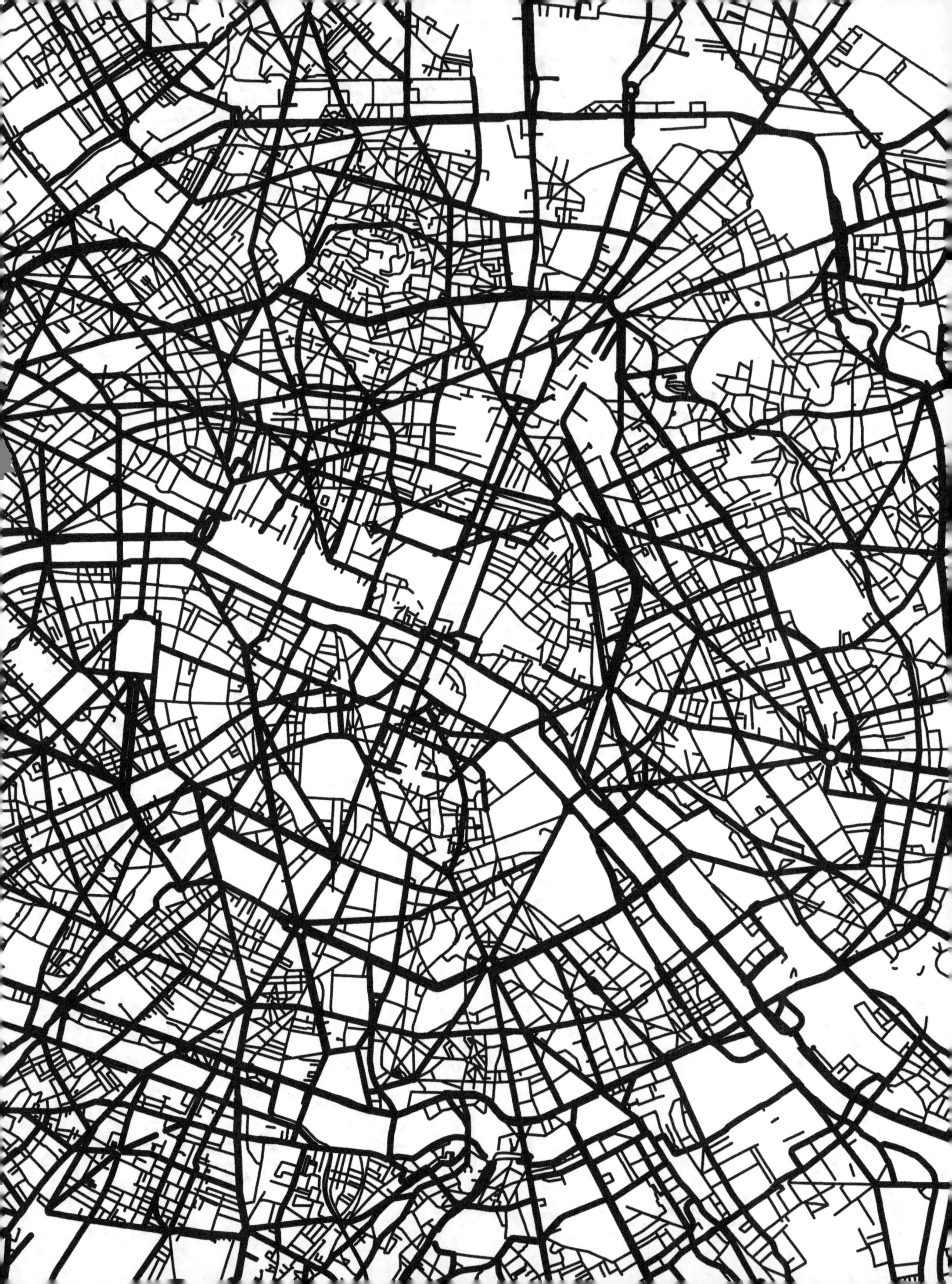

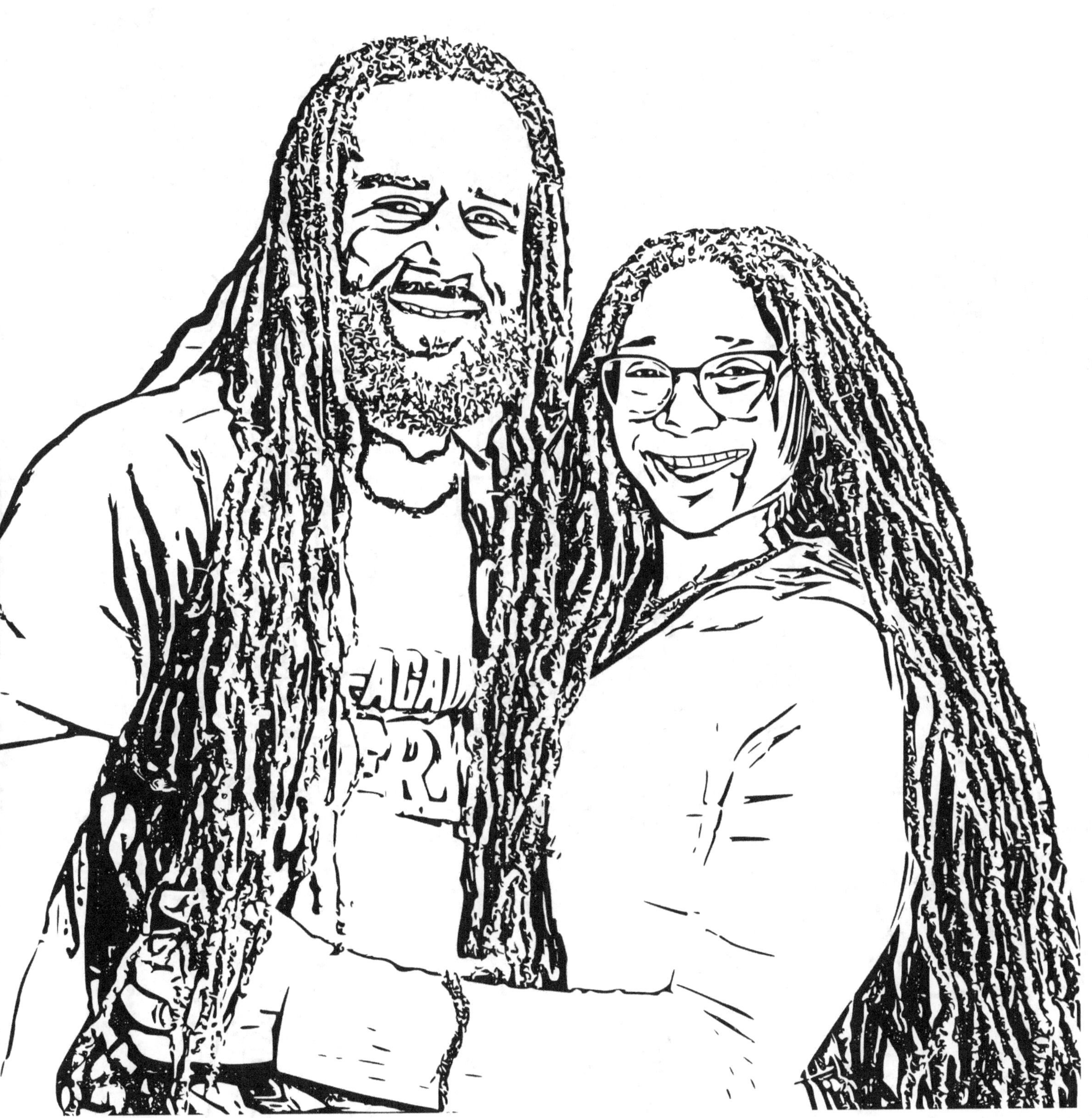
ACAD
PR

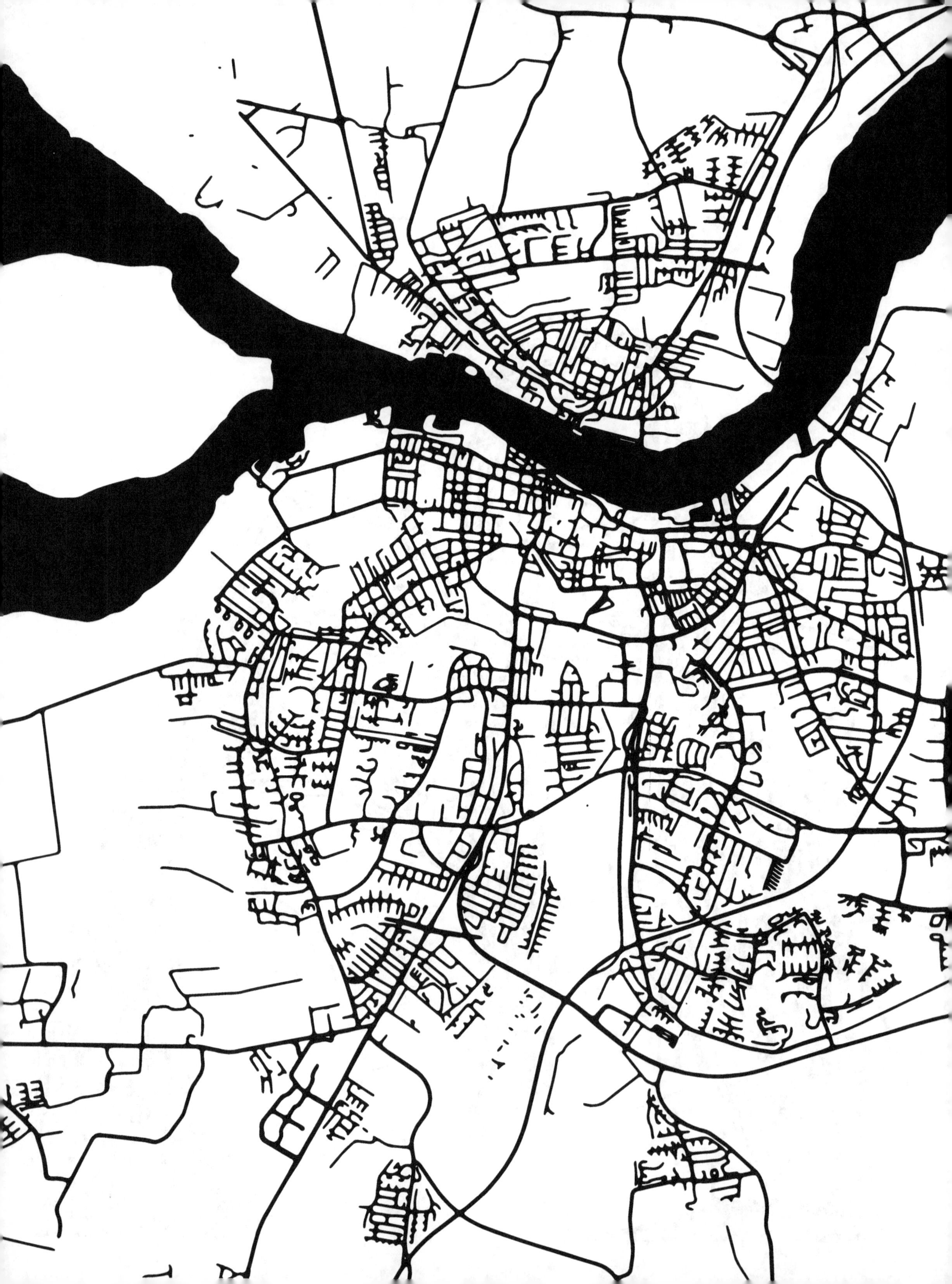

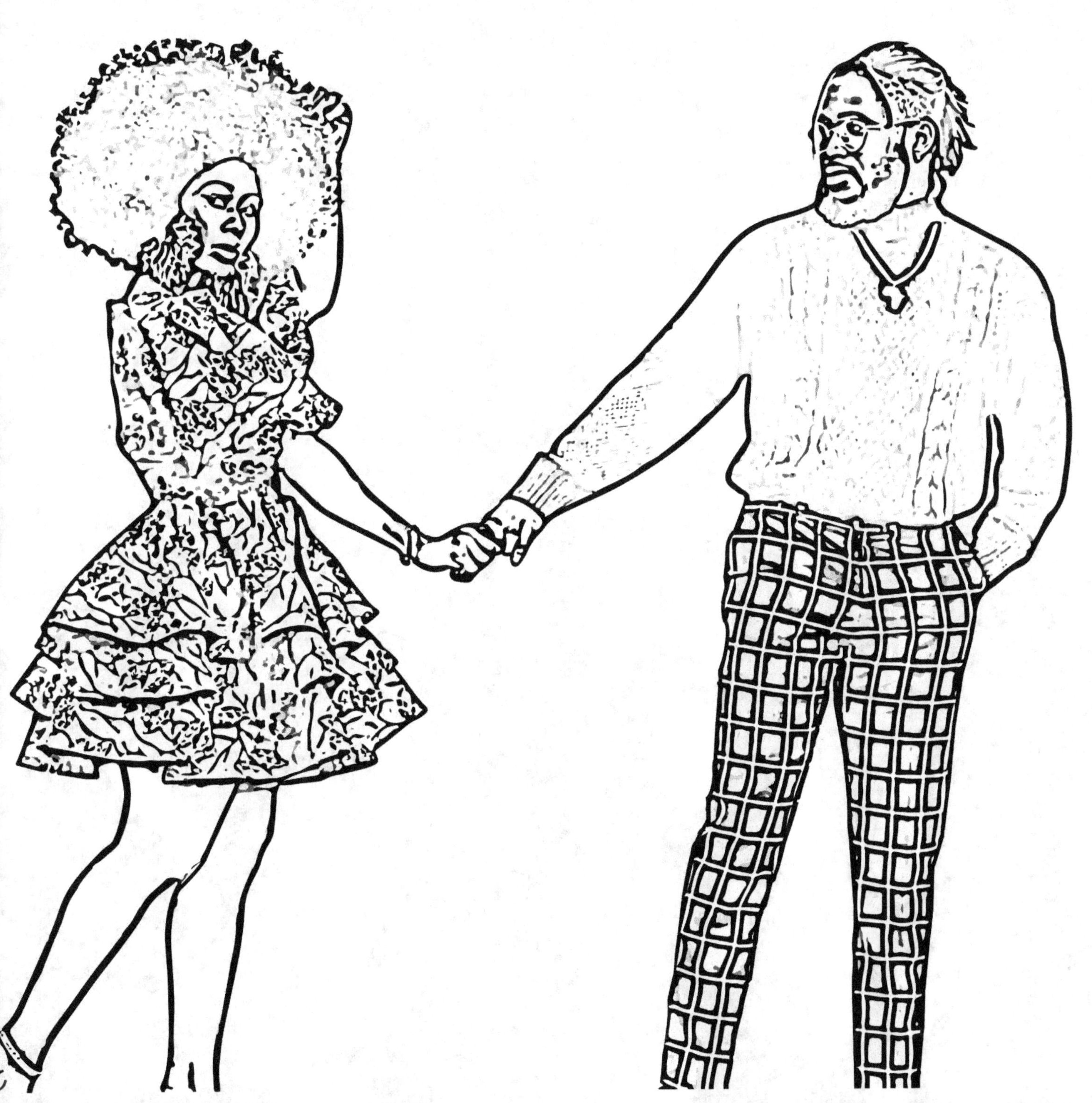

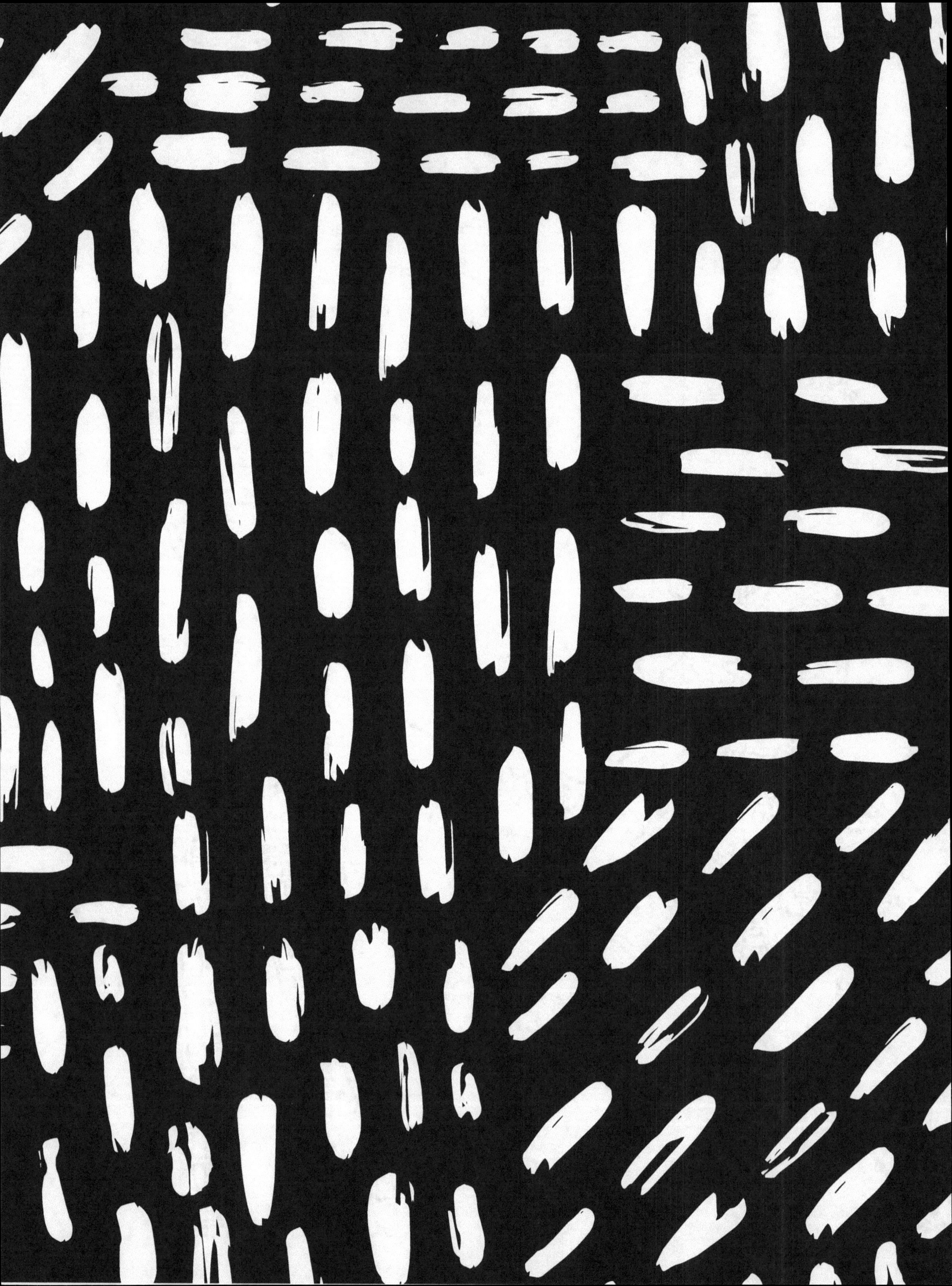

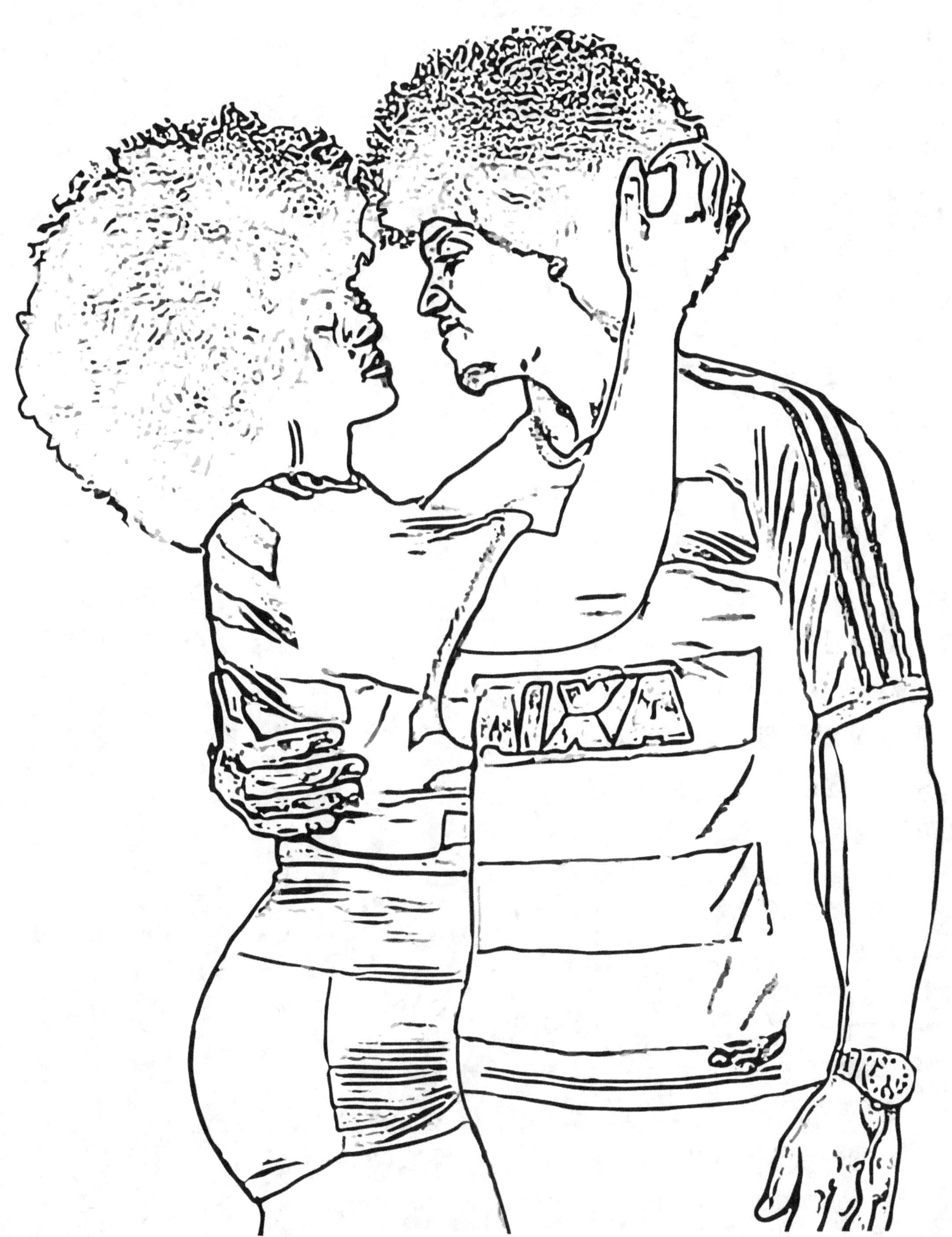

AIXA

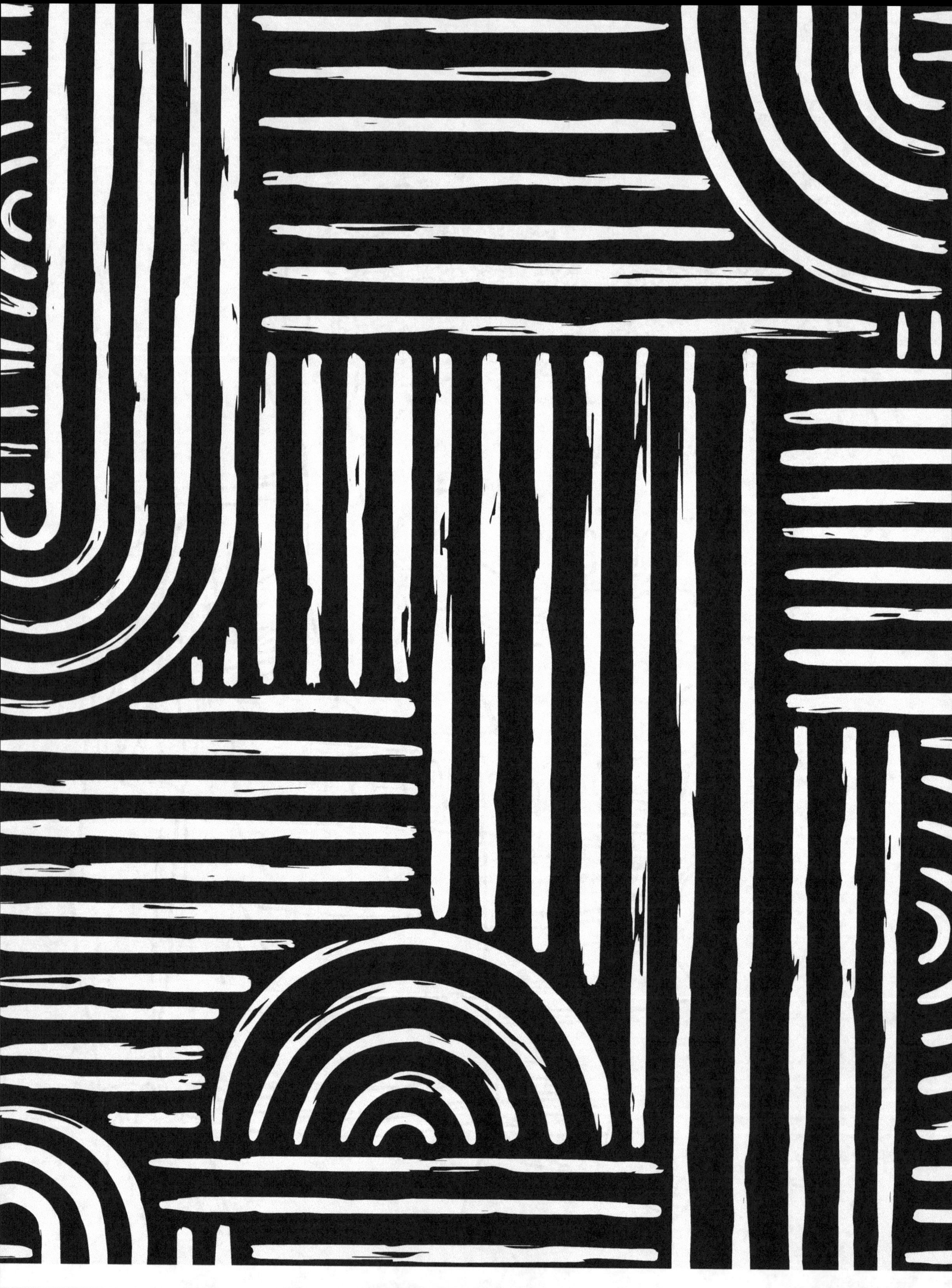

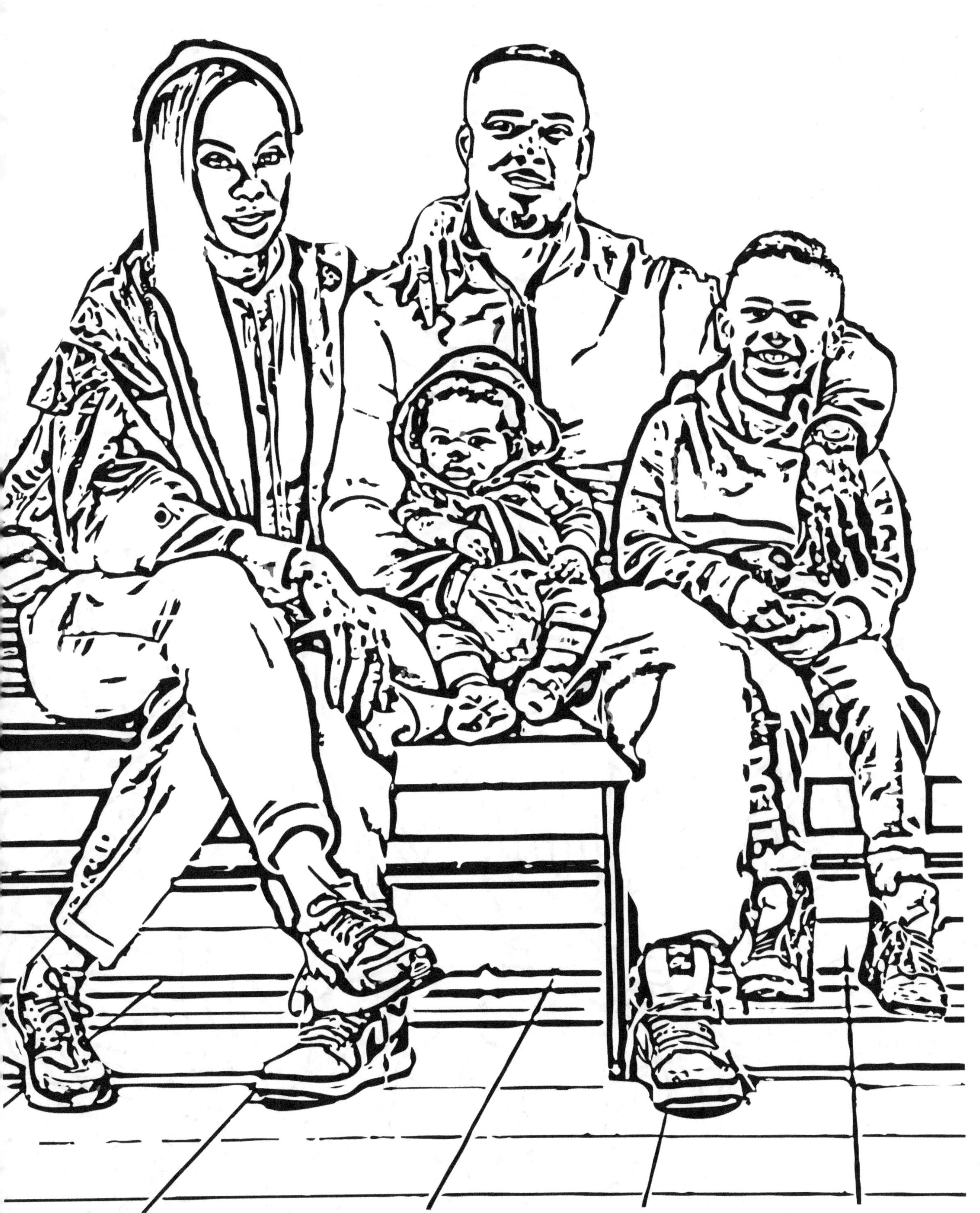

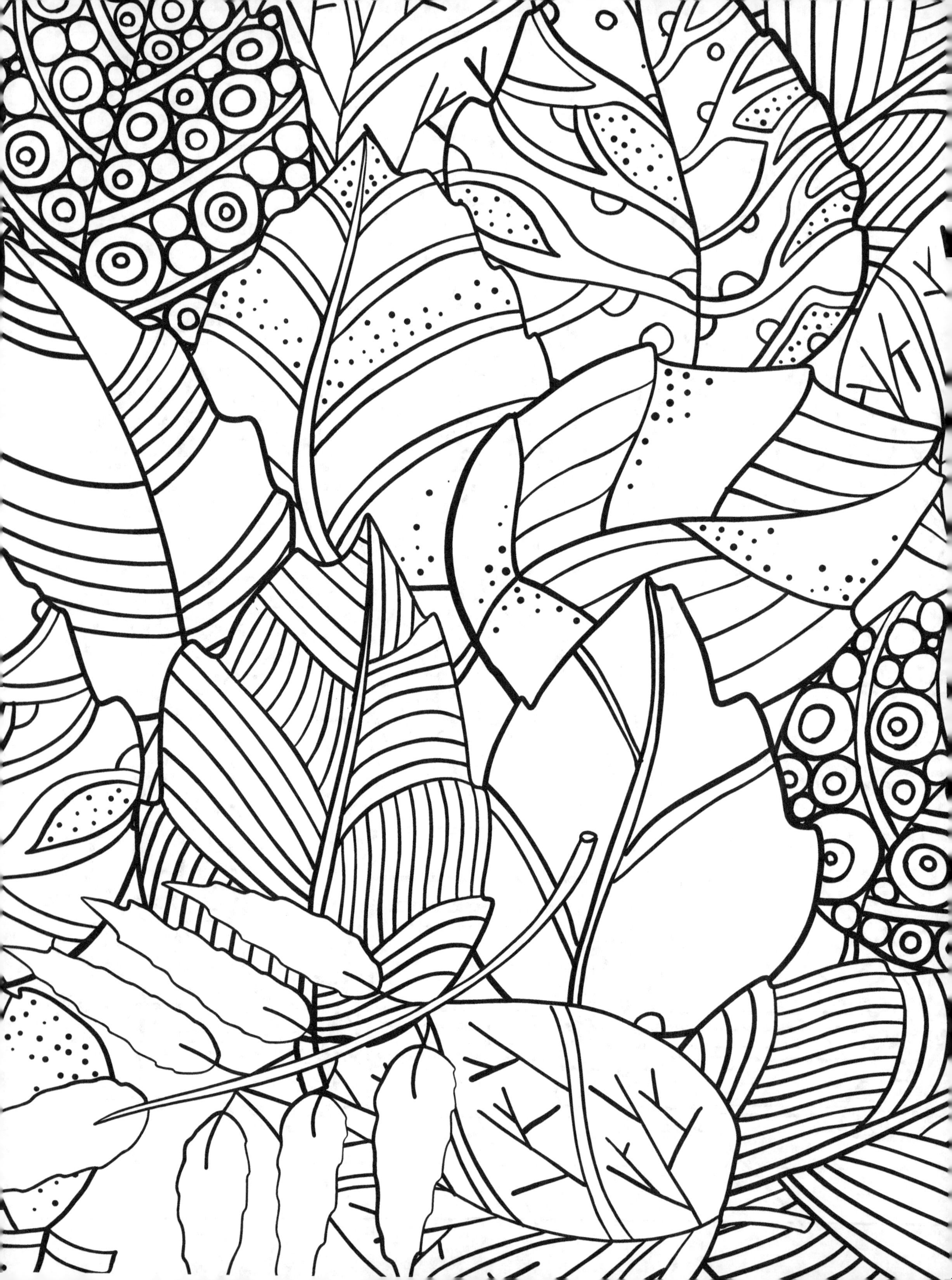

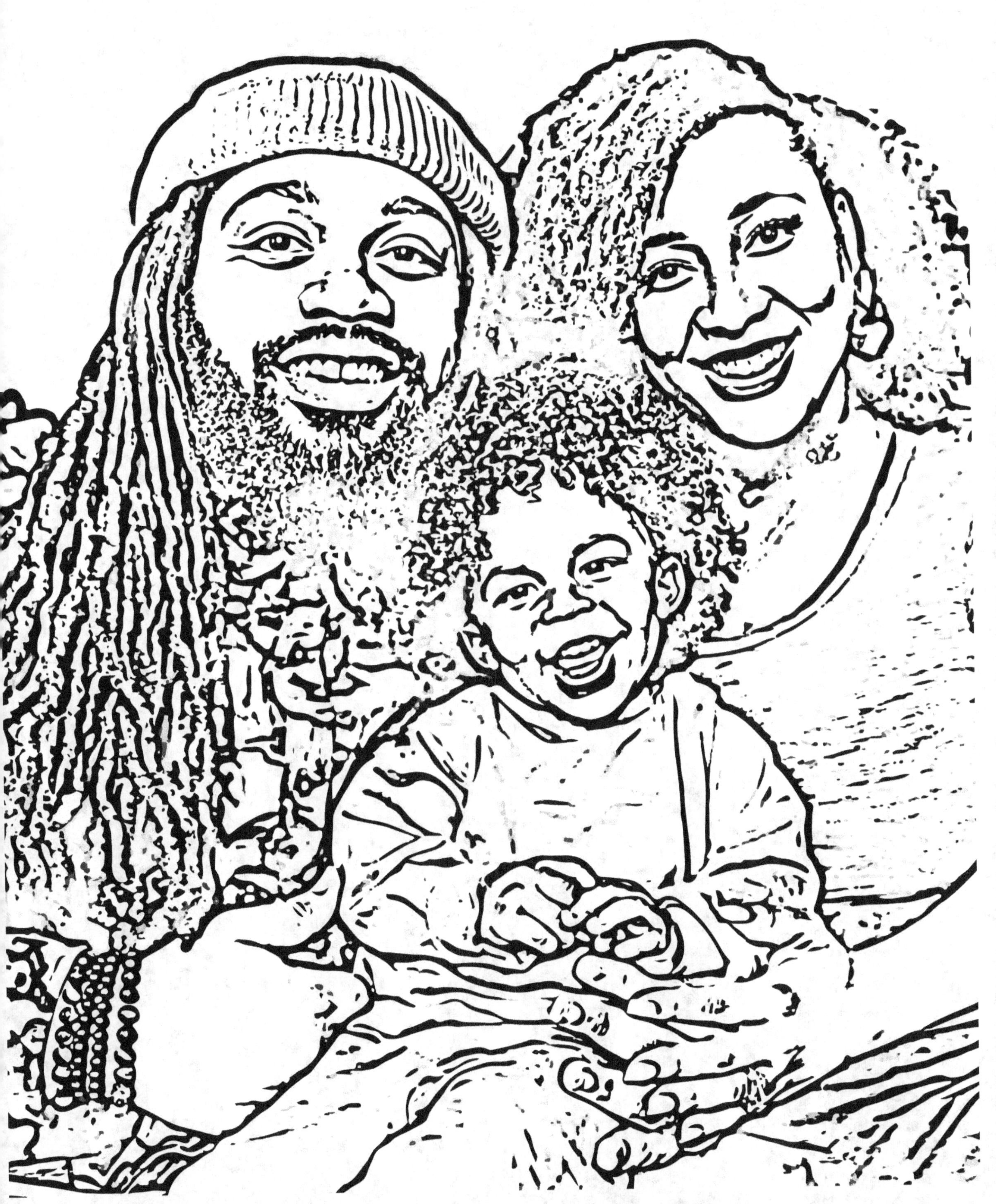

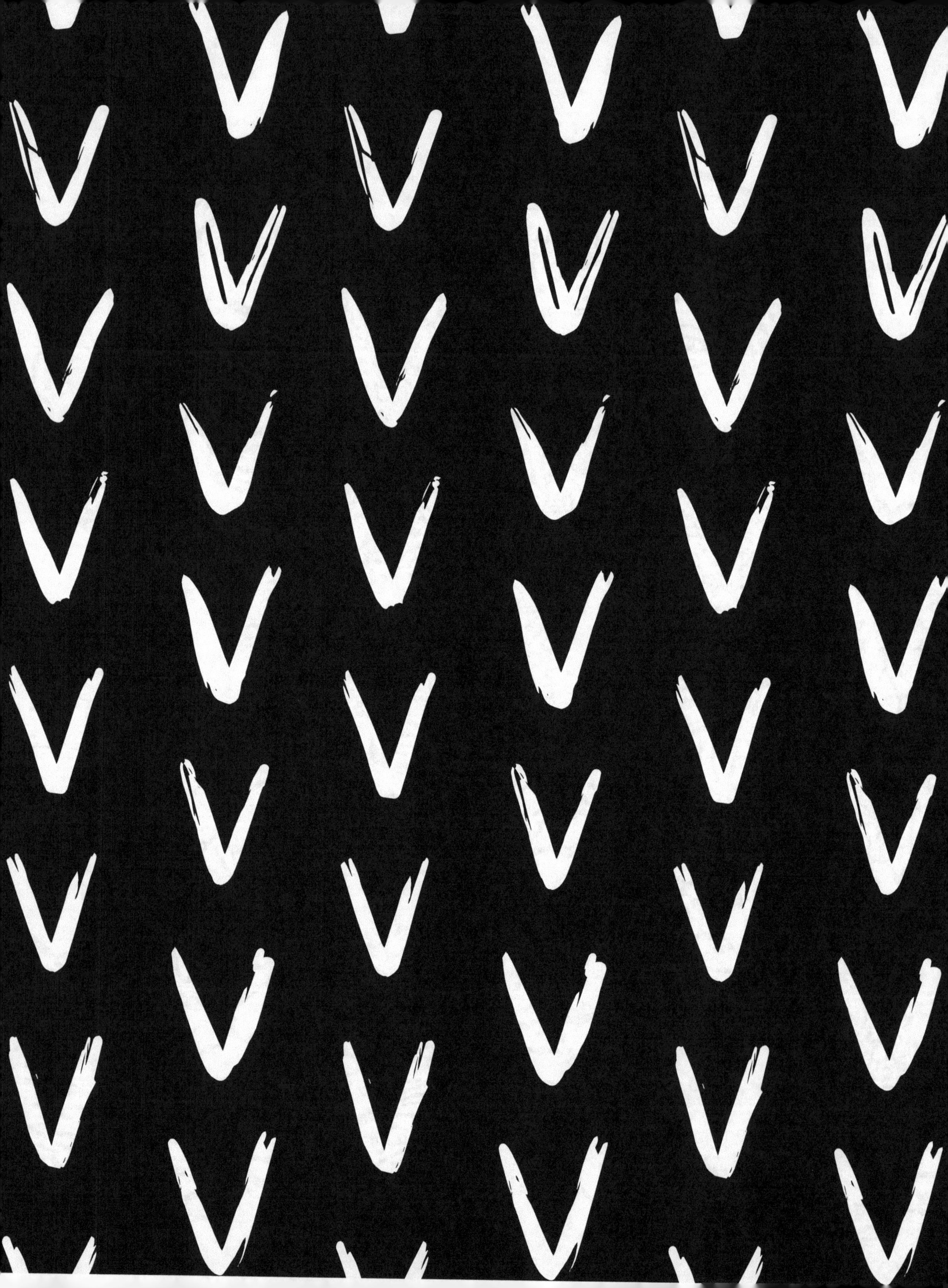

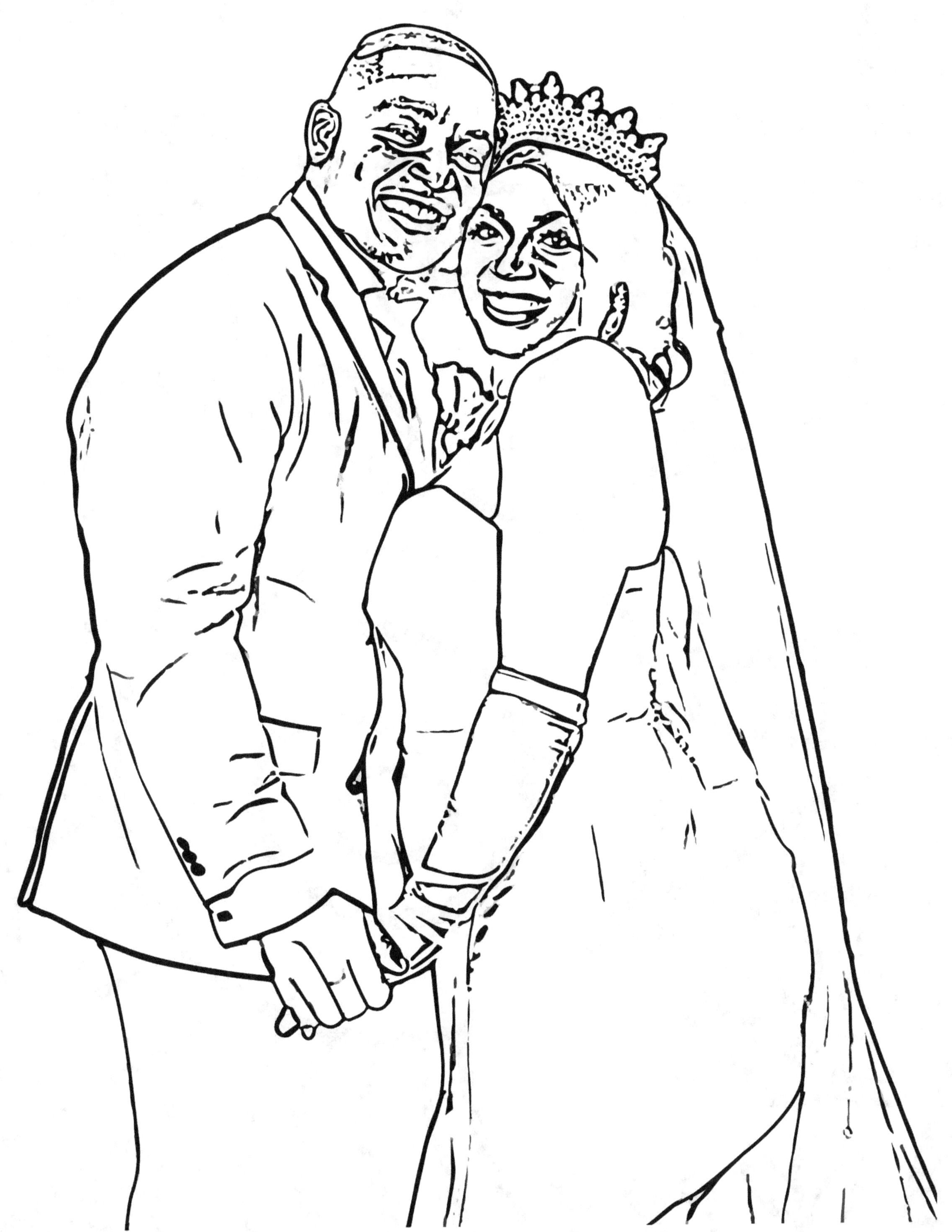

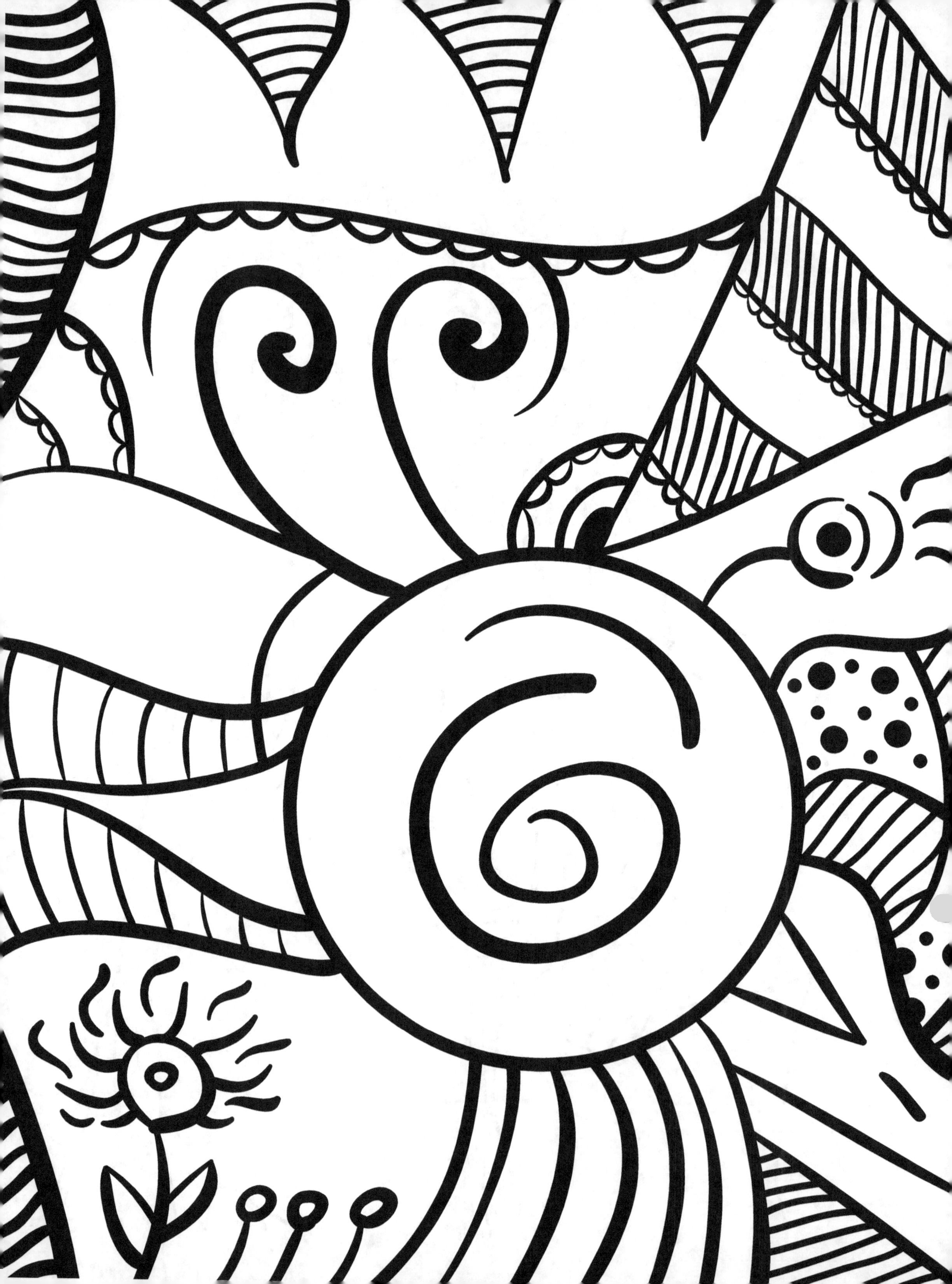

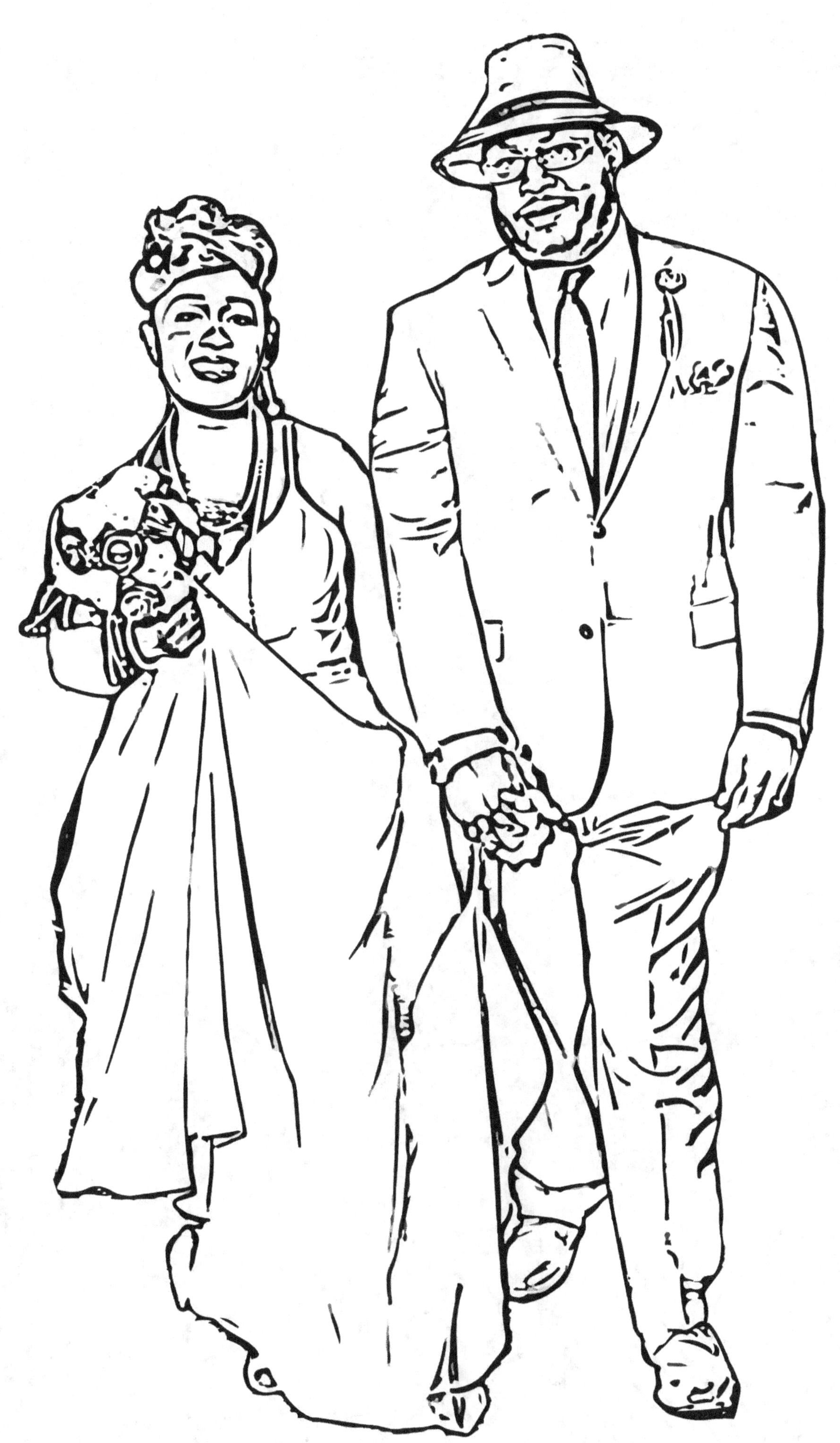

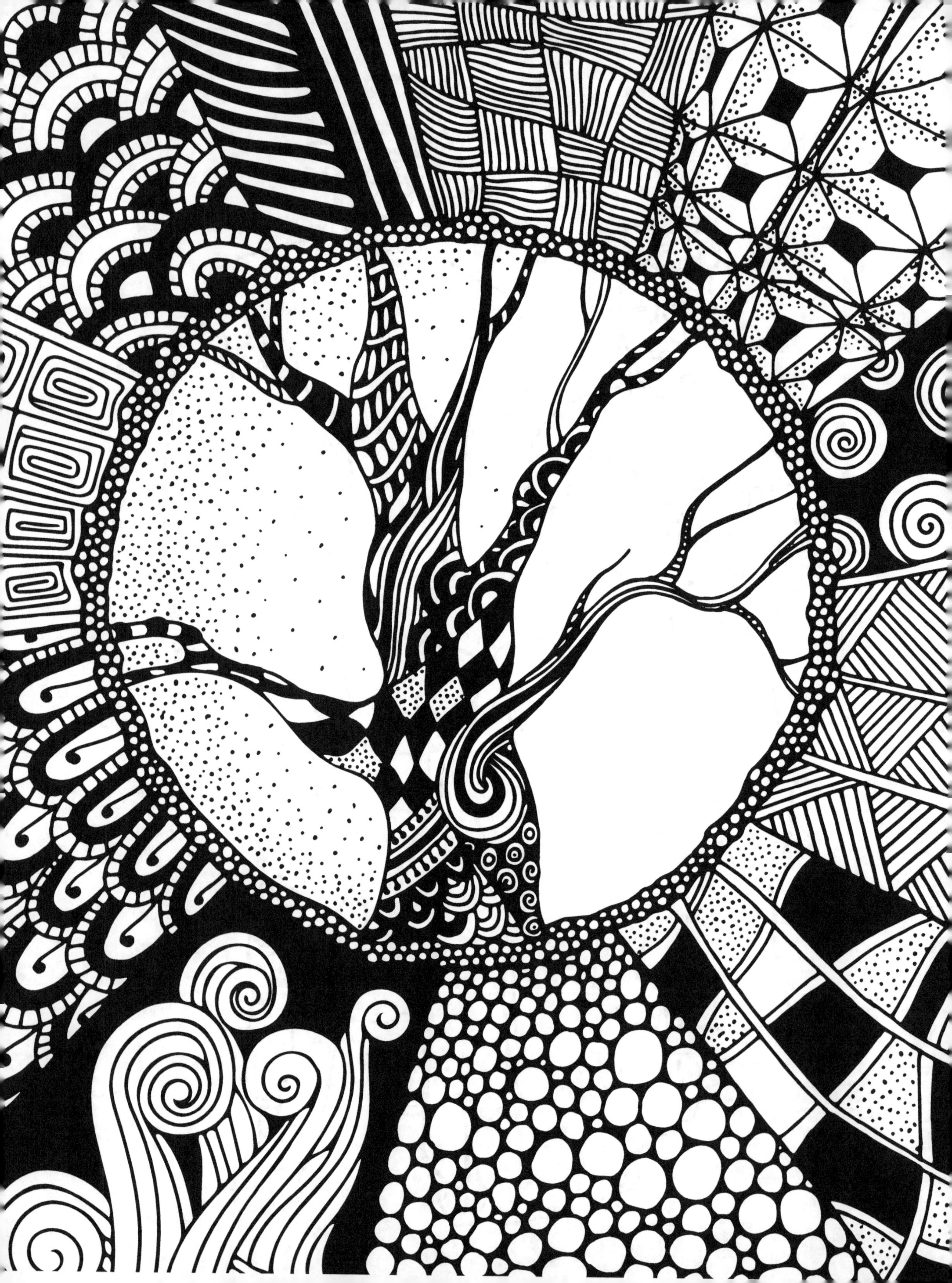

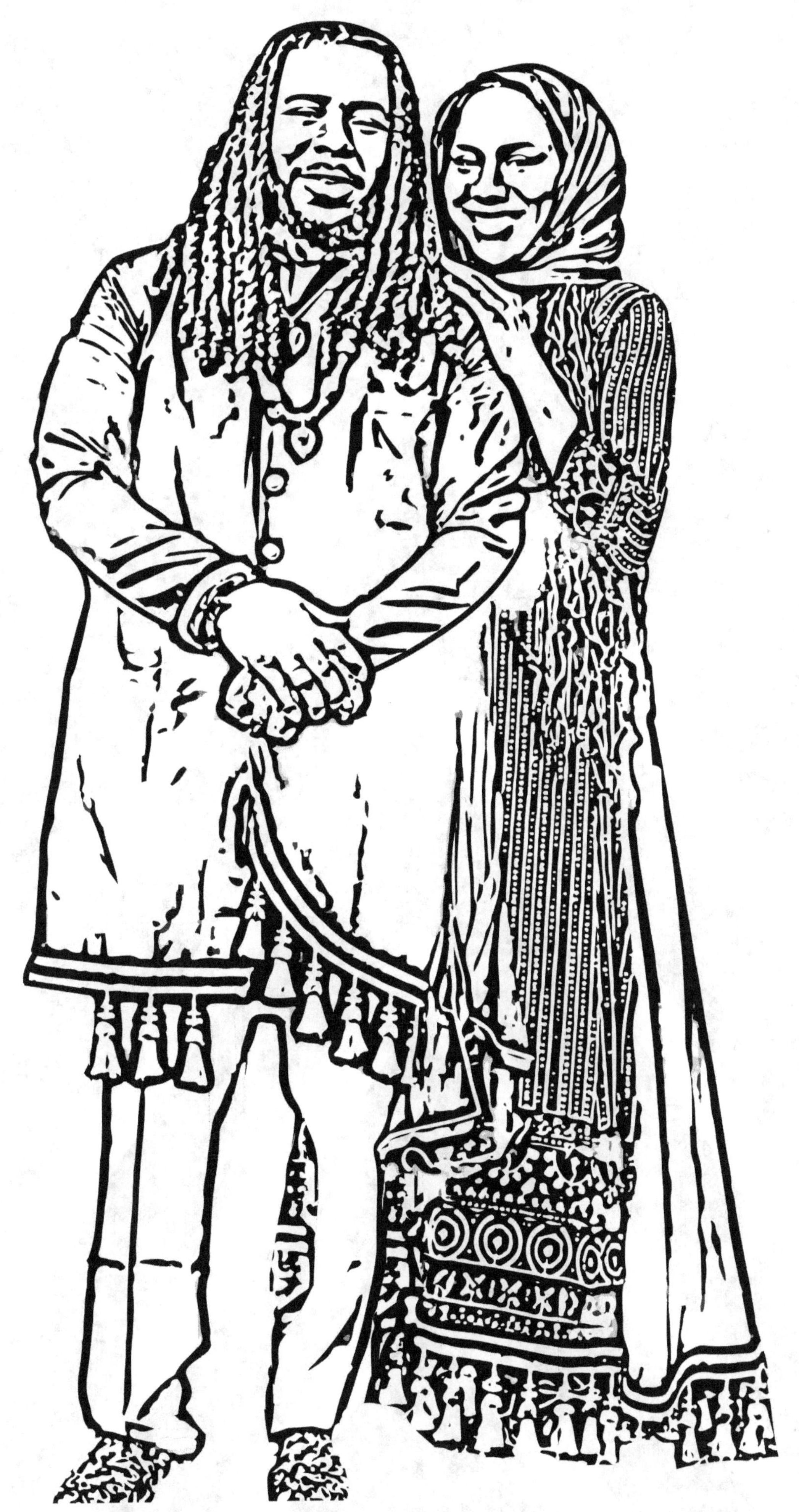

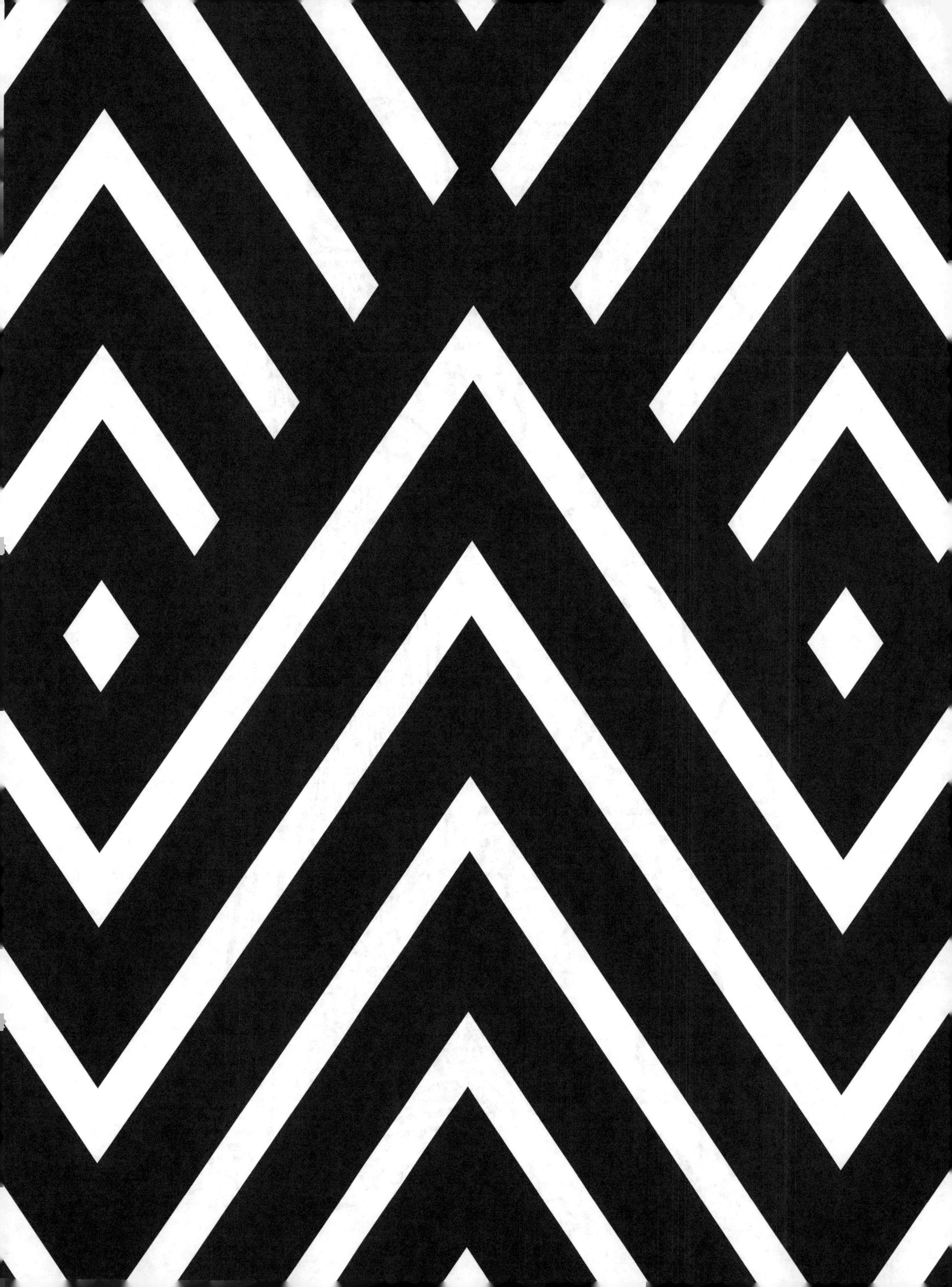

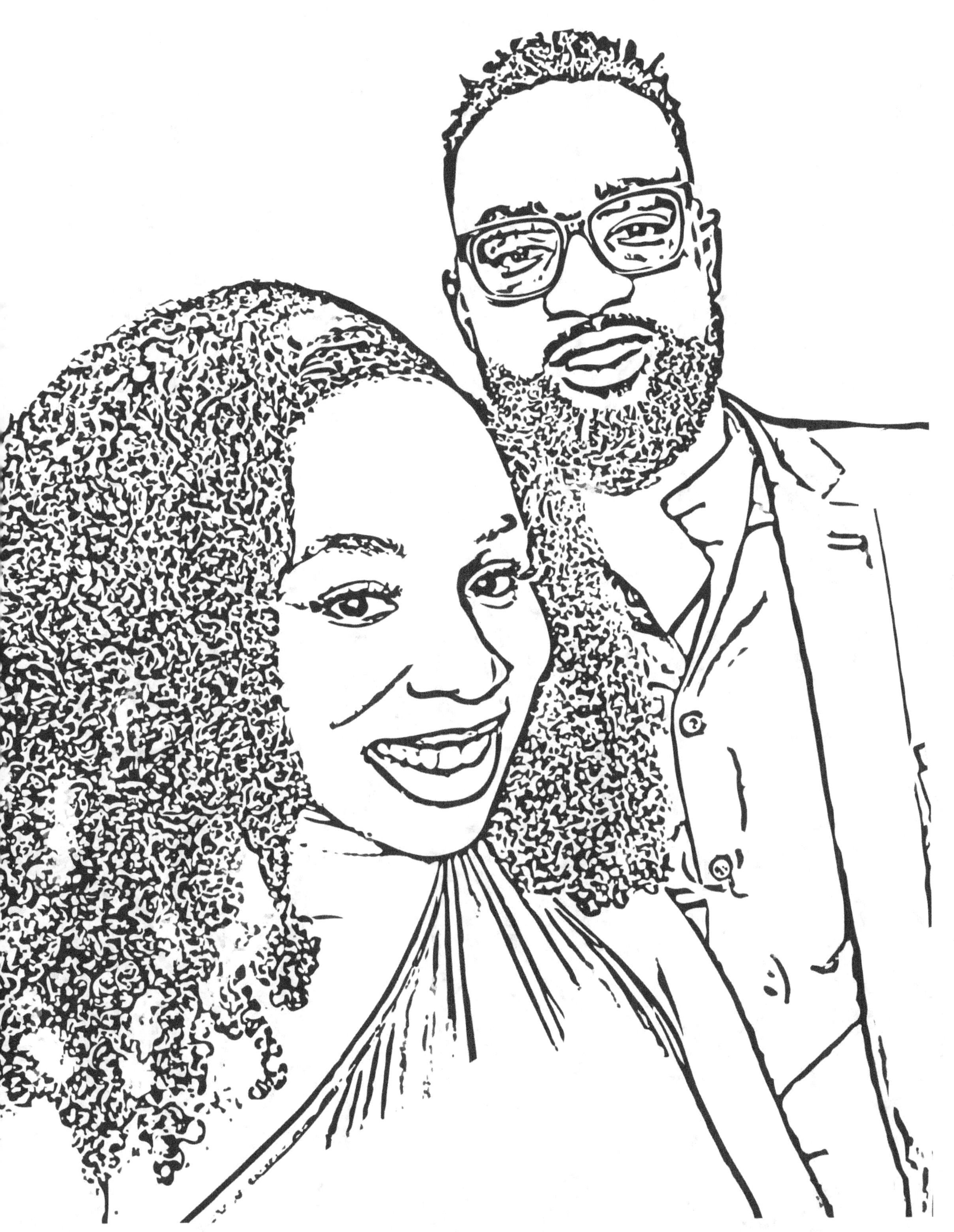

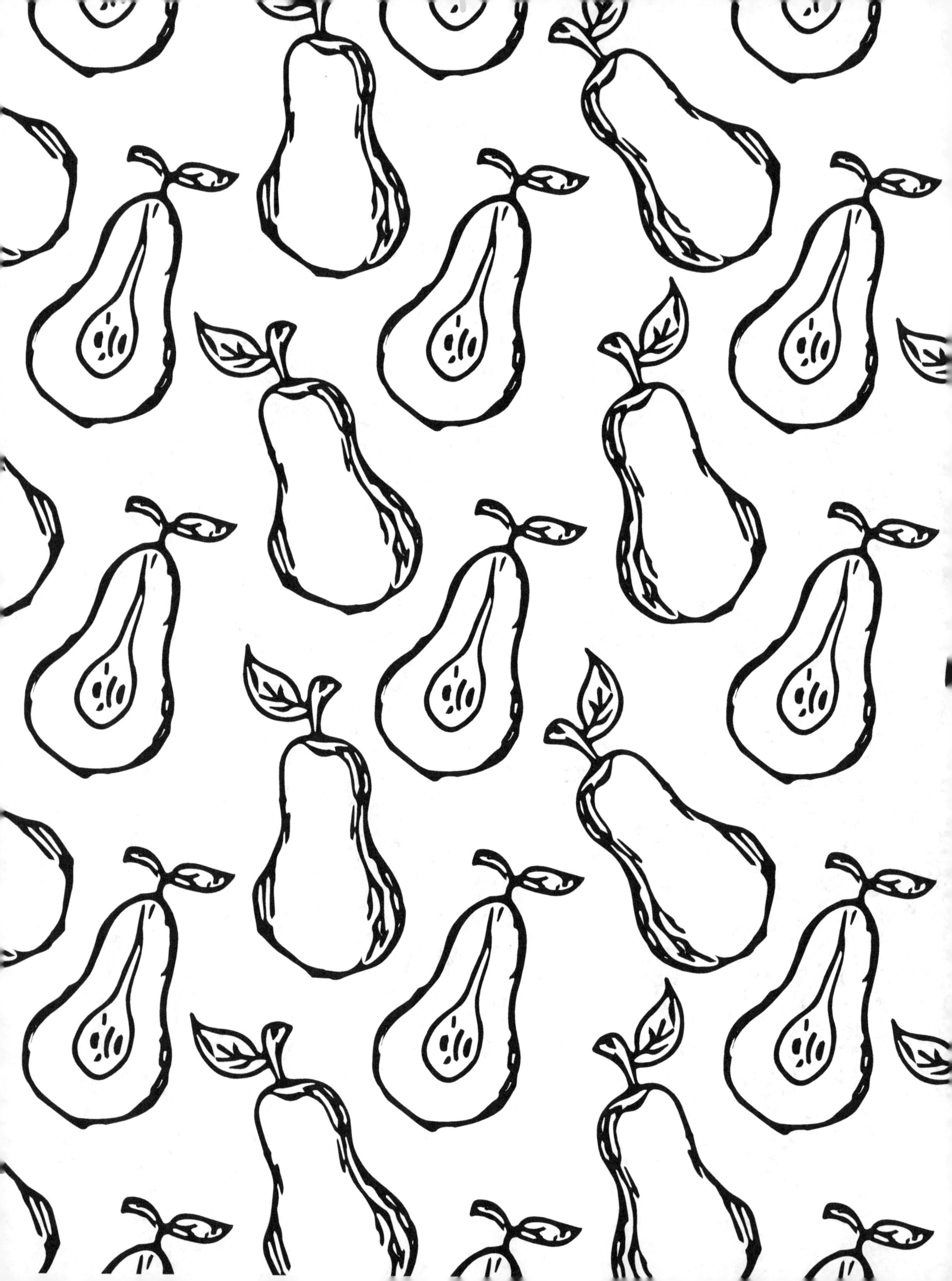

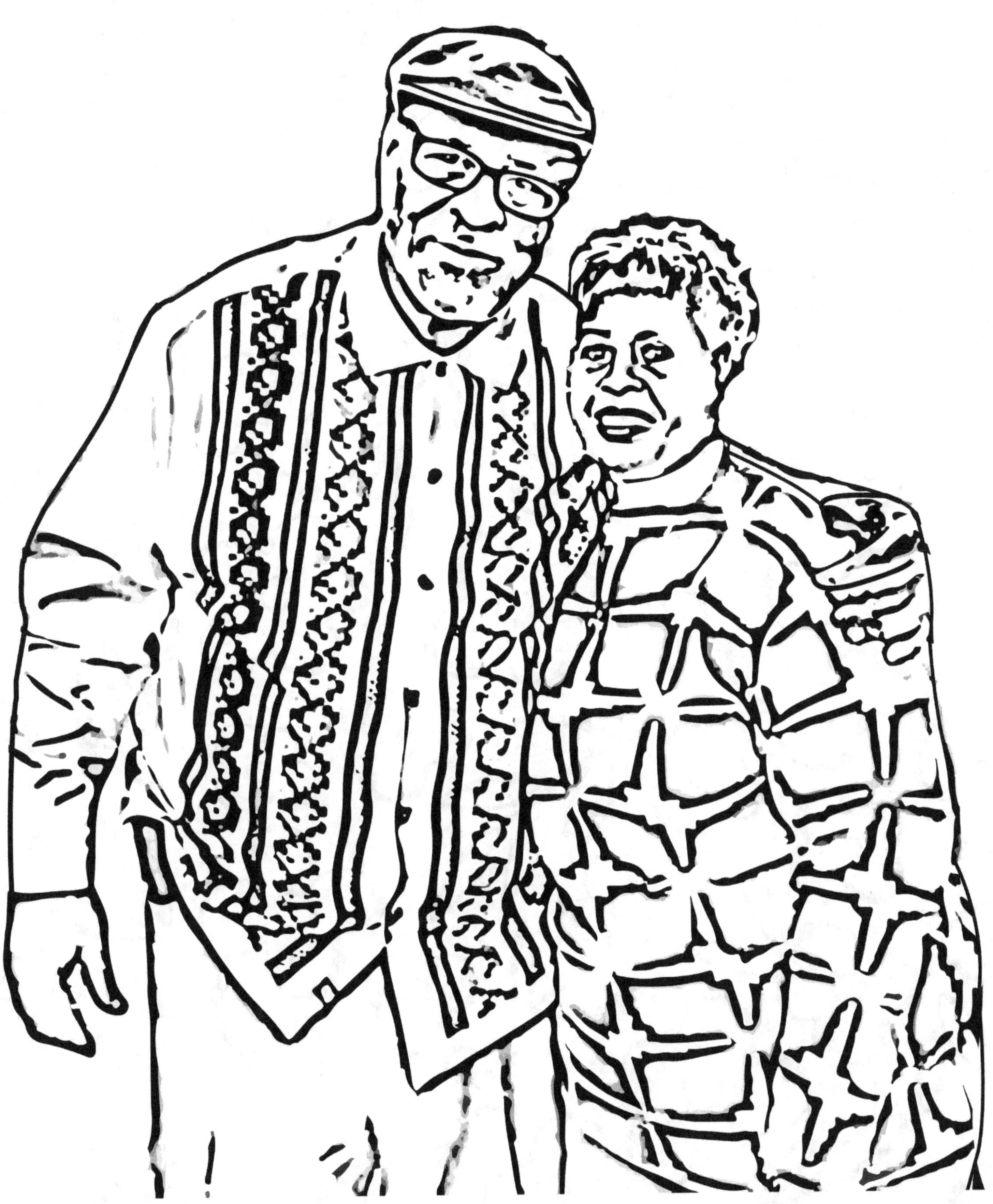

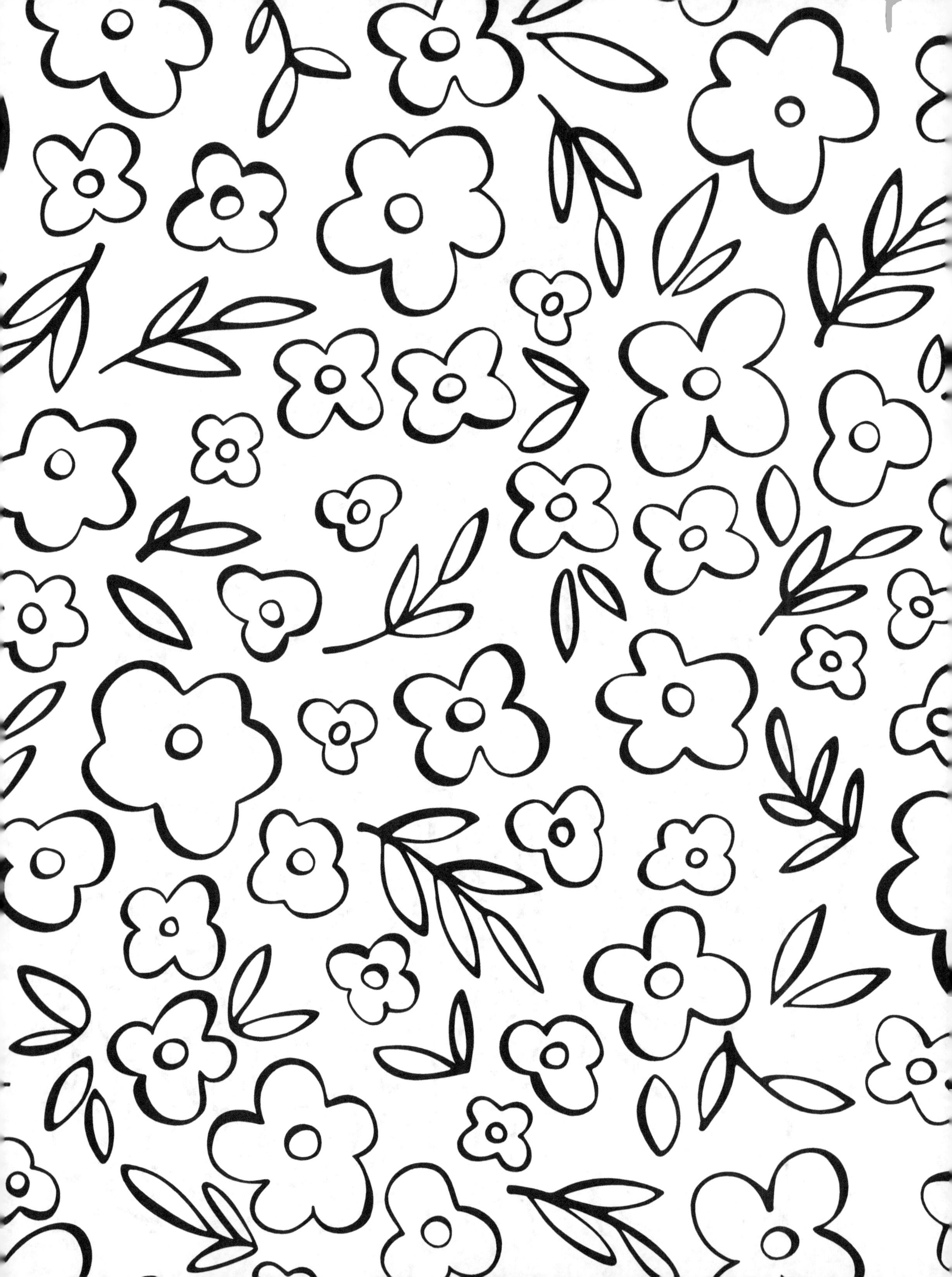

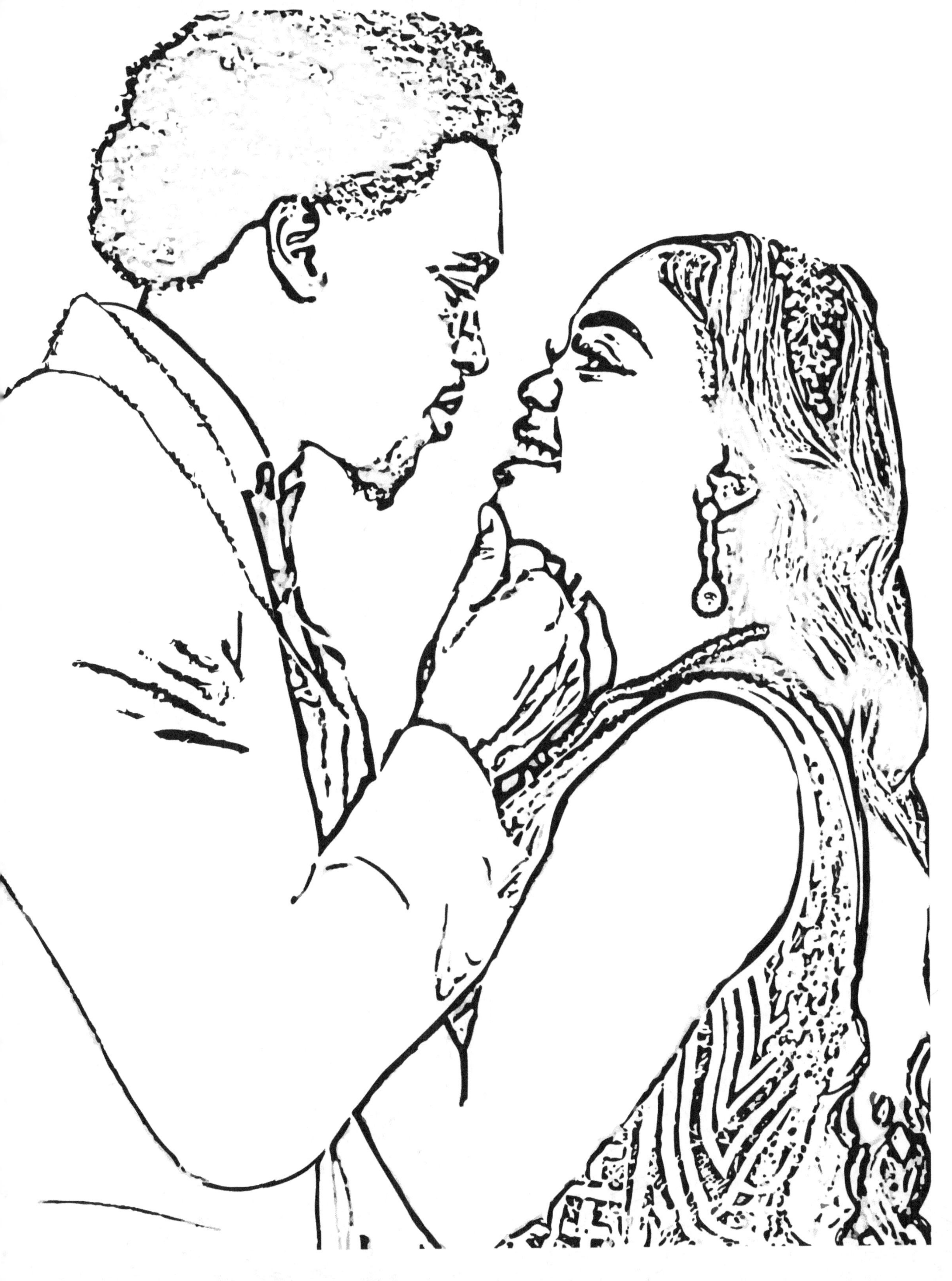

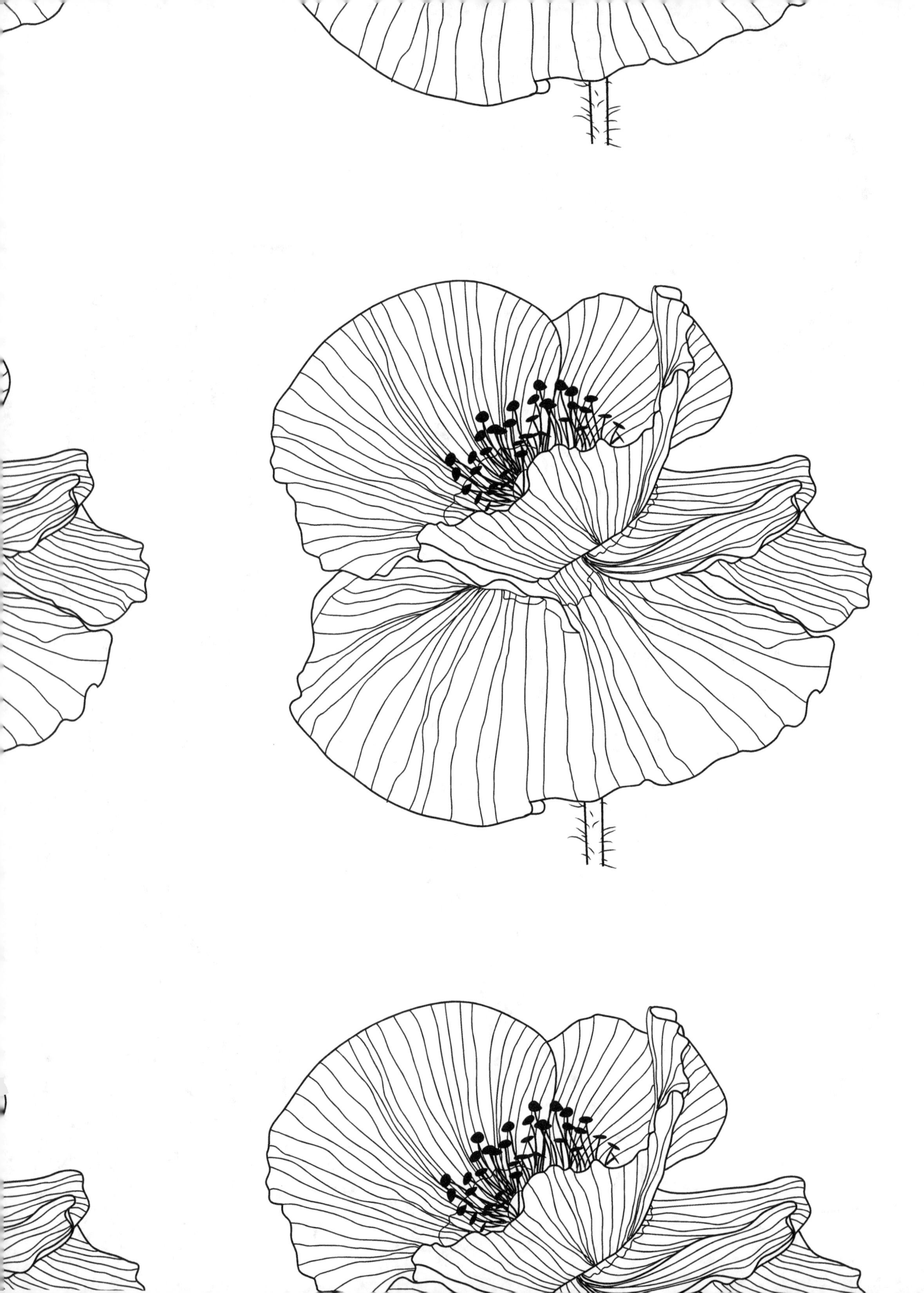

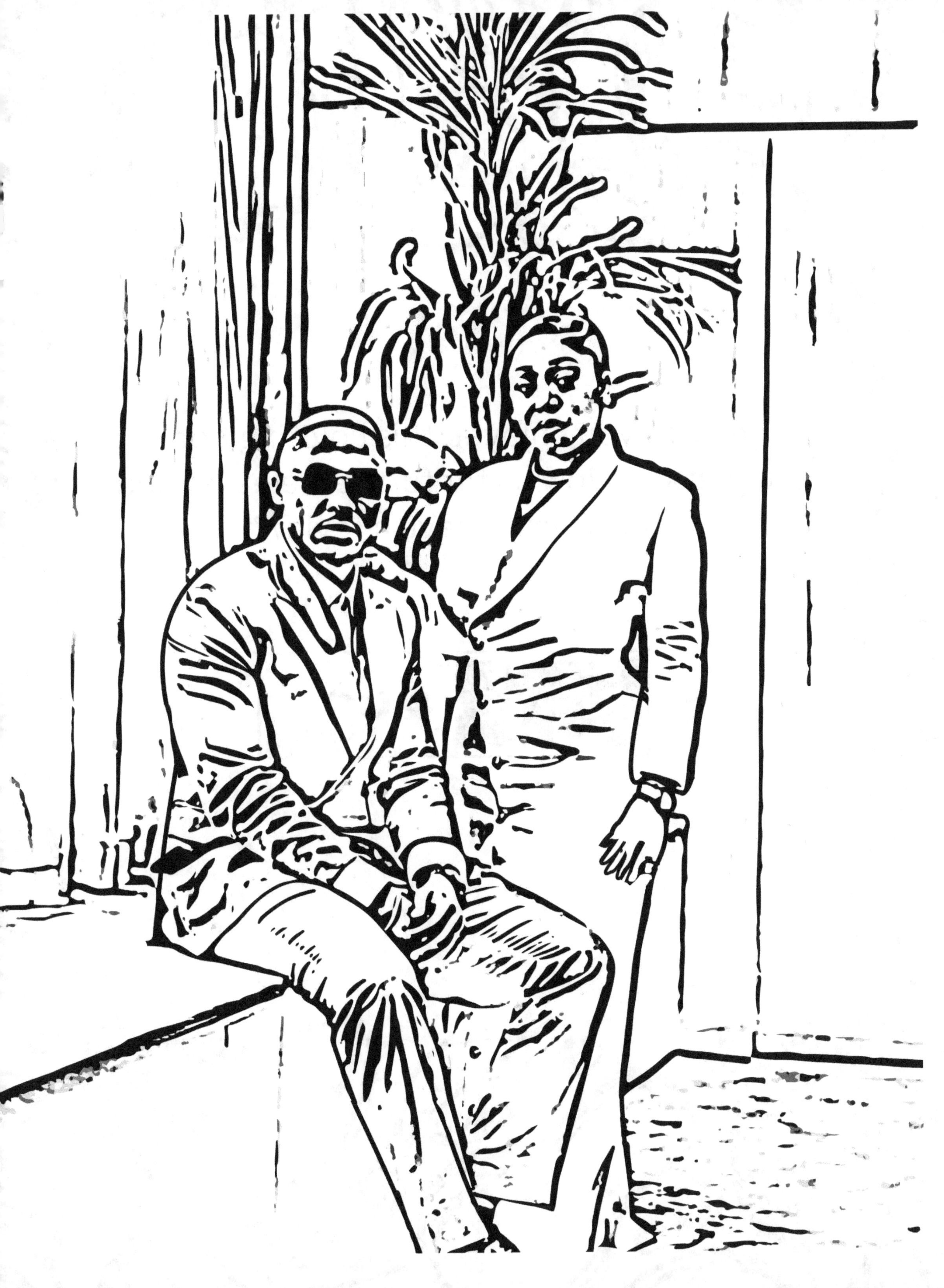

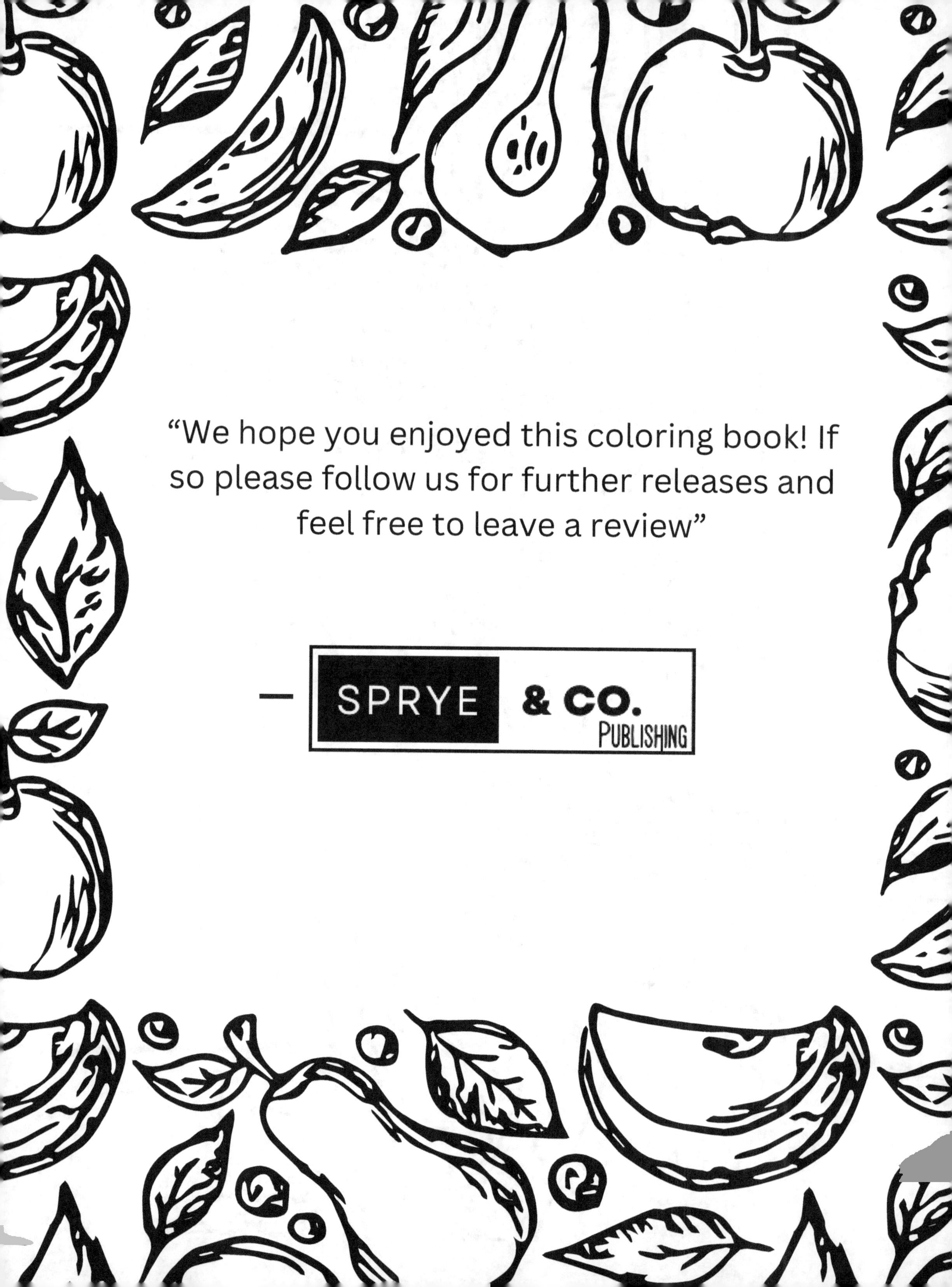

"We hope you enjoyed this coloring book! If so please follow us for further releases and feel free to leave a review"

— SPRYE & CO.
PUBLISHING